The Seven T's

Also by Judy Collins

MOVIES

Truth

Trust

Therapy

Treasure

Treat

Thrive

Transcend

The Seven T's

FINDING HOPE AND HEALING
IN THE WAKE OF TRAGEDY

Judy Collins

JEREMY P. TARCHER/PENGUIN

a member of Penguin Group (USA) Inc. · *New York*

JEREMY P. TARCHER/PENGUIN
Published by the Penguin Group
Penguin Group (USA) Inc., 375 Hudson Street, New York, New York 10014, USA ·
Penguin Group (Canada), 90 Eglinton Avenue East, Suite 700, Toronto, Ontario
M4P 2Y3, Canada (a division of Pearson Penguin Canada Inc.) · Penguin Books Ltd,
80 Strand, London WC2R 0RL, England · Penguin Ireland, 25 St Stephen's Green,
Dublin 2, Ireland (a division of Penguin Books Ltd) · Penguin Group (Australia),
250 Camberwell Road, Camberwell, Victoria 3124, Australia (a division of Pearson
Australia Group Pty Ltd) · Penguin Books India Pvt Ltd, 11 Community Centre,
Panchsheel Park, New Delhi–110 017, India · Penguin Group (NZ), 67 Apollo Drive,
Rosedale, North Shore 0745, Auckland, New Zealand (a division of Pearson New
Zealand Ltd) · Penguin Books (South Africa) (Pty) Ltd, 24 Sturdee Avenue, Rosebank,
Johannesburg 2196, South Africa

Penguin Books Ltd, Registered Offices: 80 Strand, London WC2R 0RL, England

Page 165 constitutes an extension of this copyright page.

Most Tarcher/Penguin books are available at special quantity discounts for bulk pur-
chase for sales promotions, premiums, fund-raising, and educational needs. Special
books or book excerpts also can be created to fit specific needs. For details, write Penguin Group (USA) Inc. Special Markets, 375 Hudson Street, New York, NY 10014.

Library of Congress Cataloging-in-Publication Data

Collins, Judy, date.
    The seven T's : finding hope and healing in the wake of tragedy / Judy Collins.
        p.   cm.
    ISBN 978-1-58542-495-5
    1. Grief.   2. Bereavement.   3. Loss (Psychology).   4. Violent deaths.   5. Tragedy.
I. Title.
BF575.G7C643   2007   2007013650
155.9'37—dc22

Printed in the United States of America
10 9 8 7 6 5 4 3 2 1

Book design by Meighan Cavanaugh

While the author has made every effort to provide accurate telephone numbers and In-
ternet addresses at the time of publication, neither the publisher nor the author assumes
any responsibility for errors, or for changes that occur after publication. Further, the
publisher does not have any control over and does not assume any responsibility for author or third-party websites or their content.

For Clark

For the lost ones
And for those who mourn them

Add your strength to ours, O God, so that when death
Casts its shadow, we shall yet be able to say,
"O source of blessing, you are with us in death as in life."

—*Book of Hebrew Prayer*

Spread your wings straight and catch the first morning
breeze of divine promise and hope. . . . Fly high, for thus it is
that one rises from dead thoughts into immortality.

—from *Letters of the Scattered Brotherhood,*
edited by Mary Strong

Roses are planted where thorns grow
And on the barren heath
Sing the honey bees.

—William Blake, *"The Marriage of Heaven and Hell"*

Prayer for Survivors

Dear God,
Let me stay the course on this
journey from darkness to light;
Let me shine the light of my own experience and
healing so that others who are new to this
path may see the possibility of a new and clear
Life built on surrender and acceptance.
Let me carry a warrior's banner before me
    believing I may change the power of
    loss into learning;
    taboo into transition,
    burden into blessing;
    grief into growth.
Let me use the energy and life in us to ease
the burdens, the heartache, the taboos and the
darkness of suicide and other tragic losses.
Let me be a servant of light, understanding and joy.
Let me overcome my reluctance with determination;
my fear with faith. I am lost without help.
Stretch out Your Hand to me here on the path,
and pull me toward You when I falter;
Let me not falter too long, but be back on the path
    after rest;
In conviction let me be kind;
In anger let me be swift and burn bright;
In surrender let me be rekindled by pure love.

Contents

Introduction

I was heartbroken. I was beyond devastation. I wanted to die, to pack it in, call it a day, call it quits, stop in my tracks. My son, Clark, was the light of my life, the bright, beautiful, creative boy who had survived so much, and been such a solace and beauty. Now he was gone. I could not see a way to live beyond that terrible day.

In 1992, at the age of thirty-three, after years of turmoil, alcoholism, drug addiction, and then, blessedly, nearly seven years of sobriety, my son took his life. In replicating the suicide of his paternal grandfather, James Gary Taylor, Clark went into the garage in his home in St. Paul, Minnesota, with a bottle of cheap champagne. He got into the Subaru station wagon he and his wife and four-year-old daughter had traveled in and enjoyed, put a hose from the exhaust into the window, started the engine, rolled up the windows, and died of carbon monoxide poisoning.

I knew that I had to find a way out of the darkness that had descended on me when Clark died. Yet I simply couldn't see how to live beyond the disaster of my loss. I was in despair.

Throughout Clark's life, there had been both dark and bright times. After his death, and despite my sorrow, I knew that if I didn't move toward the light, I would be forever engulfed in darkness. I began to understand that I had to fight to escape my dark decision and that life beyond tragedy had to have its beauty and peace. I fought the inner demons who promised I was wrong, who promised that darkness was all I could expect.

In 2003, eleven years after Clark's death, I wrote *Sanity & Grace,* a memoir of my experience as a witness, attempter, and survivor of suicide. I felt I had a responsibility to talk about the taboo that surrounds suicide, and shed as much light as I could on a subject about which I had had the misfortune to know a great deal. What could I do with this new and devastating information but share it?

My own particular loss came from suicide, which carries in its aftermath a unique banner of social devastation and pain. But what I have learned is that the particular silence that rings like a death knell for suicide survivors has similarities to the silences that attend other tragic losses. Though perhaps not accompanied by the same baggage of centuries of punishment and retribution as suicide, these other silences can also be devastating. I have also learned that the more we can talk truthfully about our feelings and experiences regarding these types of violent and unexpected losses, the easier it will be possible to communicate with others and to find peace and healing in our lives.

After the publication of *Sanity & Grace*, I began to speak for groups of survivors, mental health organizations, and community service groups that deal with suicide prevention and survival. I have been a social advocate all my life, speaking for the rights of the repressed, be it women's rights, children's rights, or the rights of African Americans and other minorities. I have also spoken out against the war in Vietnam and other wars that followed. In these years of surviving my son's death I have come to understand that these losses have political and social aspects as well. This struggle, truly my own in ways that were as deep and much more desperate than any I had experienced, would take me to those who were also suffering the devastation of suicide as well as other tragic losses.

Through my speaking, I have met people who have survived other kinds of devastating loss; sudden death by disease or other unexpected, shocking circumstances. Whether by suicide, accident, or being in the wrong place at the wrong time, or by the cruel logic of genetics, these lost loved ones demand of their survivors the strenuous exercise of life-enhancing acts—of walking through the fire of pain, one minute at a time, of traveling deeply into thoughts, prayers, and actions that perhaps they never would have known.

As I have shared my own story with other victims of tragic loss, I have heard voices of hope and of desperation, and stories whose honesty and candor took my breath away. From New York to the Rocky Mountains, from Florida to the coast of California, I heard the truth.

And as they say, when you've heard the truth, the rest is just cheap whiskey.

I began to emerge from the dark place of my own loss and come out in the light, and wonder how it was even possible that I could arise from my own suffering in a state quite the opposite of loss and pain. How could I again have joyful days? I learned some of the answers, and now, years later, I have begun to sift through what this process was. What would the recipe look like if I could print out a formula, a method, point by point, step by step, of getting through the awful, ugly, devastating, demoralizing experience that suicide had imposed on me?

Suicide and catastrophic loss are democratic destinations; you can't make too much money to suffer from suicide in your family; you cannot be too poor to have a family member suddenly taken from you in an inexplicable and perhaps violent manner. In every profession, there is suicide. Performers are no more apt to kill themselves than stockbrokers;

deaths of salesmen take place as numerously as deaths of desperate housewives by their own hands—and seemingly happy housewives. Truck drivers have incidents of suicide and murder, and teenagers too often commit suicide.

The connection between alcohol, drugs, suicide, and violent death are abundantly clear. People may create a cover story in order to "protect" the families, calling these incidents by other names that seem more palatable—heart attack, accidental overdose. There are many ways to cloud the truth. I have friends who are ER nurses and paramedics and they tell me that a large percentage of the people who find their way to emergency rooms are suffering from the effects of drug and alcohol ingestion, whether overdosing or simply over the legal limit.

Yet, in contrast to education in high school about civics, driving while drunk, safe sex practices, how to make a lemon soufflé, or recite Shakespeare; how to parse a sentence, add up a column of figures, read Italian and speak English, prevent sunburn and pregnancy, most junior high and high schools do not teach students how to spot a suicidally inclined young person; there are no classes in how to point out and treat depression, and seldom do you find a school where anyone is talking about treatment centers that specialize in alcoholism and drug addiction, or giving out information on how the traumatic losses from the results of addiction may affect our lives, or what we may be able to do about it.

If the makers of alcoholic beverages spent as much money on prevention and education as, say, the manufacturers of cigarettes have spent on education, we might have an entire revolution in alcohol-related suicides, deaths in automobiles, murders, and other associated and catastrophic losses of life. I am praying and waiting for the day when, instead of the simple injunction to "drink responsibly," there will be actual education, funded by these distilleries, about alcoholism and the effects on those who do not handle alcohol well—in lost work time and medical bills, family dysfunction and mayhem, and other terrible tragedies. Mothers Against Drunk Driving has gone a long way to educate about the effects of alcoholism. The distilleries could follow suit with education about the disease that kills so many. Lack of this knowledge has contributed to my loss, and, perhaps, yours.

I have seen and heard many others who have survived the unimaginable—the mother who lost her daughter at the age of two, when the child pulled over a pot of boiling water on herself; the son lost in a fire; my godfather, Holden, and his wife, Ann, old family friends, whose twelve-year-old son was shot by another friend in a hunting accident. How do people survive?

The groundbreaking work of Elisabeth Kübler-Ross has given us a road map for both surviving the death of a loved one and coming to terms with our own mortality. She has shown us that there are ceremonies, patterns, and precepts that can help us better understand what can and will come to us in witnessing and experiencing death. From her studies we have learned about those phases: anger, denial, bargaining, acceptance, rage, and, finally, peace.

I hope that *The Seven T's* can offer further information on navigating these stages of grief. From my own personal experience as well as the experiences of brave people I have had the honor to speak to about their losses, I have come to believe there are points along the way—stations of the cross, if you will—that can heal us more quickly, that can deliver us from the raging passages of loss and awaken our eyes to the beauty of life again.

I wanted to grieve, and remember my son. I wanted to celebrate his life. But I also wanted to live and to thrive, to go on into the next day, the next year, with my optimism torn but renewed.

There are things I have had to do, places I have had to go, and knowledge that I have had to gain about how to survive those stages. Like learning a new language, how did I put the steps in order, to pull my heart and my life out of the fire? What did I do, what did other survivors do, that made them able to live fulfilled, happy, joyous lives in the wake of tragedy?

How do people do it? How did I do it? How *do* I do it, every day?

How do we keep on healing?

When all seems lost, that is the time we must find what is really there behind the cloud of doubt; the time to transcend is when transcendence and faith are impossible.

From my own experience, as well as from the stories I have heard from friends who have gone through the worst kinds of loss, I have culled a set of tools. Together they form a kind of mantra of seven points to recall and remember as you dig your way out of tragedy and loss:

1. *Truth*

   Tell it. Regardless of how terrible the facts may be and how hard it is to talk about it, don't hide the truth about how you lost the person you loved.

2. *Trust*

   Allow it. Don't let the painful circumstances surrounding the death of your loved one keep you from talking with friends about your loss. Trust the people around you to give you the support you need, and if they cannot, find people who can.

3. *Therapy*

   Get it. Seek help, be it through traditional talk therapy, your art, meditation—whatever method you choose, or combination of those methods—but get the help you need. You must be your own advocate, and find the methods that will heal you.

4. *Treasure*

   Hold on. Don't stop treasuring your loved one. Don't let the horrible events leading to his or her death wash away all of the things that were good and beautiful about that person's life. As you let go, hold on, as well.

5. *Treat*—with Temperance and Tenacity

   Take care of your body and mind with exercise, meditation, and other relaxation-producing activities. A healthy physical life can alter chemical imbalances. Exercise and meditation in particular can raise serotonin levels in the body and improve your moods for the better. There is much you can do in your own time for your own recovery.

6. *Thrive*

   Keep living with your eyes wide open. Don't give in to the temptation to abuse alcohol or other addictive substances to blunt or blur your sadness.

7. *Transcend*

   We are in the process of learning how to live again—with joy, with commitment to expressing all of ourselves: our hopes, our aspirations, our life that is still to be lived—in celebration of ourselves as well as of those we love, those who are in our lives and those who are no longer with us.

You must. Live a life of joy, abundance, and forgiveness.

In this book I will take you through the tools I have used to do more than survive. I hope they will help you as much as they have helped me.

Judy Collins
November 2006

The Seven T's

ONE

Truth

Tell it. Regardless of how terrible the facts may be and how hard it is to talk about it, don't hide the truth about how you lost the person you loved.

Truth Affirmations

I will tell the Truth, hold it close.

I know that Truth is always the answer.

Telling the Truth frees me from regret, bitterness, and remorse.

Truth will help to heal those around me; it will brighten the shadows.

The Truth may change, over time. My experience and my process will reveal things to me that I may not see at first.

The Truth will set me free.

Death cancels everything but truth; and strips a man of everything but genius and virtue. It is a sort of natural canonization.

<small>WILLIAM HAZLETT</small>

*A*t first there was shock—shock that formed a protective cover, that shadowed the pain and covered the darkness with more darkness. This shock held the truth in its spell. I knew that in order to recover, I somehow had to break that spell.

The shock is necessary. I can see that it helped me to live through the minutes, the hours, the days and nights of loss. My son was gone, and I was in mourning, but in a kind of cushioned place. Shock is a great medicine; it keeps the pain away for a while, it helps us to simply put one foot in front of the next. I was going forward, but I was not really moving. Shock is a needed pause, when things are barely reaching you. I did the things that were necessary, helped make arrangements for the funeral, gathered my family around me, prayed, and fasted without meaning to, for I could not eat. But after the shock began to wear off, I had to let myself in on what had happened. It was then that the pain began in earnest. This wearing away can take days; it can take weeks.

But don't allow it to take years, for this can damage us and those we love who are still here to love and be loved by us.

On this journey through the mountains as well as the valleys of loss, we must have supplies—friends, mentors, food for thought, the right clothing to get us through the rough and mighty changes in temperature, in climate, in altitude.

> Truth is the offspring of silence.
>
> ISAAC NEWTON

Nature helps us with these necessities, since She often takes away our judgments, our energy, our preconceived ideas of what life is all about, even our resistance to change. We are laid low by sorrow, made ready for change. Death, and all loss, is about change. And all change forces us to face truths that we sometimes might rather avoid.

And we must have the truth.

All great truth begins with the smallest, the most private, most personally anguishing details about our loss. In their secret, ancient darkness resides our light, our escape, our freedom, if we can but face these things. I knew I had to do this in order to do more than survive. I had to do it in order to live.

I had suddenly awakened to find myself on a terrible new

shore, thrown up like a bottle with no message, no instructions on how to live on this sad island where I had landed. Like others with whom I have spoken since, I was convinced there was no help; I was convinced no one understood. I was sure, as perhaps you are as well in the wake of your own tragic loss, that no one could see me for what I was: devastated. Alone.

When you have lost someone whom you cherished, whom you looked to for sustenance, for love, for friendship, no truth seems enough. Perhaps the person you loved was a close relative, a son or a daughter, or parent. No matter what the age of the person you lose, if you have lost someone unexpectedly, violently perhaps—and tragically—this sudden loss is going to change you. No matter how you resist the changes, they are going to come. The loss may plunge you into an abyss, over a cliff, suddenly taking your heart and your energy. Your only weapon will be your honesty, your truth, and your story.

At first the only thing I had *left* was the truth. We have to tell our own story, and find our own peace and our own light on this path of loss. I somehow knew I was never going to recover if I didn't let myself in on the problems, the reality of where I was.

My new name, "suicide survivor," floated down like a black veil, covering every previous accomplishment and happiness with darkness, accusation, fear, and the hollow ring of useless, empty words: "I didn't know, I could have helped,

I should have done something, why didn't he reach out, tell me what to do?"

That was when I had to learn the first truth of suicide and other tragic losses.

FIRST TRUTH: LOVE IS UNENDING

I had to learn a new language, the emotional language of loss—the new way of talking to Clark, of seeing him, hearing him, of communicating from this side of the grave. He was there, I am here; but we are not done with our dialogue. It has new words, a new face, a new voice. This new language is the language of dreams and wisps of hope; it has the newness of pain, and the ancient sound of weeping, but it is the language I would now have to master if I was to do more than survive.

Stephen Levine, in his important book *Who Dies?* says that when we lose someone dear to us, all there is left to do is to love them. He describes the way in which death forces all barriers aside, leaving us free to hear and speak the clear, direct call of love without fear. And love is the first word in the new language.

Perhaps this truth can only emerge once we are further down the path of grief; often in the beginning stages of recovering from a great loss all we can do is suffer our pain and confusion. But at some point we must allow the understanding that we can simply love someone whom we are mourning with all our heart, all our soul, all our strength. At first, it is certainly not clear that there may be blessings, gifts, light after dark, and peace to come when we are lost in the deep turmoil of losing someone we have loved. Time will heal us, yes, but we must first walk the path of healing, touching all the markers on the way to our recovery.

Yet I urge you to see your way to the simple truth that the love does not end.

In our guilt lies the thought that we might have changed the outcome. Guilt is a self-destructive tool. When I lost

Guilt is playing God.

my son I knew that I did not want to self-destruct; my son had already done that. I had to find ways to bypass this guilt, to temper it, to change it from dark to light, from self-destruction to self-protection.

And although there are deeply different emotions and taboos as well as reactions of guilt that must be overcome in the case of a suicide, the first lesson with all tragic loss is the same—that there was nothing, not a change in attitude, not an appearance by us at the crucial instant, not a prayer or a breath that could have altered things in that fateful moment, or before or after our loved one's death by any means.

In order to come to some kind of peace with my loss, I have found that I must understand that life is not always under my control. In the Bible, we are told that man has control of all the animals on the planet, all the living creatures.

But the reality of our fate is very different. I can seldom have much effect on the thinking and the actions of others, although I sometimes wish this were not so. The truth is that fate intervenes at every turn. Fate, like life and death, is not under our control.

There is a saying in the recovery programs for families of alcoholics and addicts: "I didn't cause it, I can't control it, and I can't cure it." This is a good practical set of beliefs for all of us to maintain, as we can become emotionally ill if we believe that we are responsible for controlling fate. I cannot force my family or my friends to live life on my terms, to follow my advice, to do it "my way." We have all had the experience of trying to force a family member into treatment, into marriage, into divorce, into calling more than once a week, into not calling more than once a month! We are never able to force people to do what we want; even our children are resistant to sound advice at times. We can only do our best.

> The truth is our teacher.
> Tell the truth and you will be
> healed and help to heal others.

In the case of suicide, as with all sudden and tragic loss, you can be sure that your unreturned phone call did not set off the process, your unanswered letter did not pull the trigger, your half-expressed love did not push the person over the edge. You did not cause the accident, the incident, the blur of sudden circumstances that came to play in that moment when your loved one, either by his or her own hand or by the hand of fate, left the planet.

TELL THE TRUTH,
BUT NOT TO HURT OTHERS

When my son died, I had to tell the truth. But I also had to be careful that in doing so I was not hurtful to others. I had to be careful to be kind, to refrain from statements that might have brought pain to others. I had to pray for others who I thought might be responsible for my son's death even as I might feel rage. I had to pray in spite of myself.

In the case of a tragic loss, a suicide or an accident that takes the life of someone we love and is caused by someone else, it is particularly easy to blame others. But the blame will only add to the pain we feel. In overcoming our grief and loss, we want to solve problems, not create them.

When I lost my son, pain was the last thing I wanted to inflict on anyone. I only wanted to be clear, to be healing to myself and to everyone involved. When I traveled down that deep path of grief and truth, I sometimes brought back the flowers of light, truth, and revelation. I wanted desperately to do more than survive.

I knew my son was suffering, and searching. I knew that he could take his life and I remembered my own attempt at fourteen. I knew he did not intend to hurt his daughter, his wife, his mother, his father, his friends. I understood that he was ill, and that what possessed him to take his life was something I could muse upon, could rail against, could hate and fear and tear my heart over. But I could not blame him.

I was not angry.

I was destroyed.

Also, I, too, was an alcoholic, unable to stop drinking, fearing that if I could not stop drinking (which I *could not*, for twenty-three years), I might complete the act of suicide. But I felt rage at the condition of loss in which I found myself, the condition of terror and abandonment—rage at fate, at those who did not help my son when they might have; rage at the turn of fate that put him at risk on that day, in that place. I knew my rage was threatening my very sanity.

The only thing that could heal me was to turn that rage into love. There will be truth in the anger you feel toward the person who has left you—or those who you might blame for the loss—but sometimes this is not the truth to speak to yourself or to others. Speak instead of the overriding love you felt.

As the days went by after the death of my son, Clark, I could feel the arms of my husband, Louis, around me, feel his love for me and his concern for me, as though he were trying to hold me back from the abyss that yawned before me. I didn't tell him that he could not hold me back, but only hold me, and love me, because I had to go deep into that void, down into that dark place, through the center of that terror, in order to get back. I knew he loved me, and that he had loved my son. I didn't know very much in those first few days, but the miracle was, I did know—and this is not always the case—that when I returned from that abyss, my husband, lover, and friend of many years would be there for me, to hold me, and to continue loving me, as he had before my son left us. And I knew that for both of us, it would test everything we had felt and known and hoped for each other and for our relationship.

But at that time I let the truth of my own isolation remain unsaid. My husband somehow knew I would come back to him. The people who were surrounding me with their love and support in my time of mourning knew this too.

SEEKING REDEMPTION IN THE AFTERMATH OF VIOLENCE

A suicide is an act of violence—to oneself, and to one's friends and family, yet the person who takes his or her own life is in such emotional pain that they have difficulty realizing how violently those left behind will be affected.

The cold violence of suicide is echoed in many other types of violent deaths where there is a victim and a perpetrator. Serious spiritual questions arise. Though the perpetrator, the guilty drunk driver, the mentally deranged murderer, is arrested and put in jail, there may remain an aching feeling that justice has not been done. And if the person who committed the crime is still out in the world, how can the family and friends of the victim feel peace?

Only the inner journey can lift the spell of tragedy from our shoulders.

Here we might look to the absolutely forgiving actions of the bereaved Amish after the murder of the high-school girls in Pennsylvania in the fall of 2006. This quiet, isolated community, whose quaint dress and life habits are for the most part shielded from the light of the press and international attention, had lost five of its young women, mostly under the age of fifteen, to a rampaging murderer. After these murders, with more victims still hovering near death, the community invited the murderer's family into their homes and their hearts, crossing the river of pain with the bridge of their spiritual discipline.

These ceremonies—prayer, forgiveness, and acting from the outward signs of inward grace, as the Catholics put it— even if not felt—can help the healing. The example the Amish set for the rest of us is powerful.

In these situations it is important to remember that the pain does not really have to do with the guilty party. It is only *your* inner journey that finally can lift the spell of tragedy from your shoulders.

In 2002 I performed in a play called *The Exonerated* in

New York City. *The Exonerated*, written by Jessica Blank and Erik Jensen, is the story of six people on death row, some of whom had been there for decades, each of whom had always claimed innocence. Through the course of the play, each of the six is exonerated by new information and forensic evidence, much of it obtained by lawyers from The Innocence Project, a group of lawyers who search the DNA and trial records of questionable convictions.

The director of *The Exonerated*, Bob Balaban, invited me to appear in the off-Broadway play in the part of Sunny Jacobs, falsely convicted and exonerated after nineteen years in prison. Jill Clayburgh opened the play's run in a performance as Sunny, who was, in real life, a slight, pretty blonde who spoke of her experiences with eloquence and humor. (The play was taken from direct interviews with the six exonerated, as well as from the words of the arresting officers, jailers, and lawyers involved in their cases.) Over the next two years, Sunny's life was captured on stage by many other actors, including myself, Ms. Clayburgh, Marlo Thomas, and Mia Farrow. For the parts of the men who had been exonerated, Tim Daly, Aidan Quinn, Alec Baldwin, and others alternated the roles, sending chills through packed houses every night for the year and a half run of the play. Danny Glover, Brian Dennehy, Aidan Quinn, Delroy Lindo, and Susan Sarandon played in the film of *The Exonerated*, which was aired on Court TV following the New York run. The film was shown in a commercial-free presentation, unprecedented on Court TV.

The story was riveting as well as disturbing. In 1976, Sunny Jacobs was twenty-six. Along with her four-month-old daughter Tina, whom she was nursing, and nine-year-old son, Eric, Sunny and her boyfriend, Jesse Tafero, the father of her infant daughter, were traveling from Florida back to their home in Texas with Walter Rhodes, an acquaintance who had offered to give the family a lift. They were headed out of Broward County in Rhodes's car when they were pulled over by the state police at a routine checkpoint. Police discovered Rhodes was on parole and asked him to step out of the car, at which point Rhodes pulled a gun from under the front seat and began firing, killing two officers.

I asked for strength that I might achieve;
I was made weak that I might learn humbly to obey.
I asked for health that I might do greater things;
I was given infirmity that I might do better things.

PRAYER OF AN UNKNOWN CONFEDERATE SOLDIER, FROM *The Oxford Book of Prayer*

There was a dramatic car chase with the children and Jesse and Sunny screaming in the chaotic ride until the officers' gunfire stopped Rhodes's car. When the police caught up with them, Rhodes accused Sunny and Jesse of the murders of the two policemen. Rhodes understood the system from his previous time behind bars. He made a plea bargain (he took three life sentences in exchange for telling the authorities that Jesse and Sunny were guilty). The only witnesses were dead, and there was no one to corroborate Sunny's and Jesse's pleas of innocence.

Every night as I sat on the stage reading Sunny's words and listening to the play unfold, I would think, that could have been me; I could have been that girl in that car with a lover and a near stranger, someone crazy and wild. And dangerous. Young and foolish, in the madcap days in my youth, or anytime, for that matter—it could have happened to me, to any of us.

Sunny and Jesse, with no money and poor legal representation, were treated as guilty from the beginning. After spending fifteen years in a separate prison, Jesse was executed in Broward County, where the electric chair malfunctioned and it would take thirteen minutes for him to die while smoke billowed from his ears and fire poured out of his head.

Ten years after the murders, Walter Rhodes admitted under oath to the killings as he lay dying from cancer, confirming that Sunny and Jesse were innocent. Nevertheless, Jesse was exe-

> They say if you want to dig two graves, contemplate revenge.
>
> ANONYMOUS

cuted five years after Rhodes's confession and Sunny spent a total of nineteen years in prison, most of them on death row.

The Innocence Project took Sunny's case in 1999, and in her new trial, she was found not guilty.

When she got out of jail, Sunny had little besides her five-foot-five frame and a family who had supported her emotionally throughout her ordeal, caring for her children and trying to visit whenever they could. She had used yoga and meditation to get her through those rough years, and continues to teach and practice yoga. Sunny would later say that her desire to turn a pile of manure into flowers had kept her alive and sustained her belief that she would someday be free again.

Scott Turow, a lawyer and author of many successful novels, served on a committee in Illinois to evaluate the death penalty. *The Exonerated* was performed for this committee, and Scott told me that his ideas about capital punishment were changed, in part, by seeing the play. He voted for a moratorium to be put on the death penalty in Illinois. Among the other evidence made available to the members of this committee was the stunning fact that as many as one in seven people on death row is innocent. Turow wrote an article for the *New Yorker* magazine in 2005 in which he described how his feelings about the death penalty had changed. He had come to the conclusion that no matter how you felt about capital punishment, you couldn't bet a man or a woman's life on one in seven.

I've told this story because for those who have lost someone in a violent manner, it is important to identify the need for vengeance and not to let it cloud your judgment. Perhaps there will never be a guilty one named—this doesn't at all diminish the love you feel for the person you have lost.

Forgiveness may be difficult, but forgiving and going forward in our lives is one of the ways we heal. The perpetrators of our sorrow may live or die, but our suffering can only lift from the inside out.

When you know the truth of being, you are the absolute monarch of your own life.

EMMET FOX, *Around the Year with Emmet Fox*

LIES THAT LIVE DOWN MANY GENERATIONS CAN POISON EVERY FAMILY MEMBER

Families often feel the repetitive dance of tragedy in their histories. Be it genetics, cancer, alcoholism, depression, heart problems, or just fate in its mysterious path, life can repeat patterns. Many people respond to these tragedies with silence—as if not knowing about it or talking about it will bury the sadness once and for all. It won't.

In the introduction to *The Best American Mystery Stories of 2005*, Joyce Carol Oates writes:

"There is no art in violence, only crude, cruel, raw, and irremediable harm, but there can be art in the strategies by which violence is endured, transcended, and transformed by survivors. Where there is no meaning, both death and life can seem pointless, but where meaning can be discovered, perhaps even violence can be redeemed, to a degree."

Don't let silence prevail in the wake of tragedy.

Peace will only come once the violence—and the sadness—are exposed to the light.

TRUTH IS THE LIGHT

When I was drinking I was often preoccupied with thoughts of suicide, and had I had a gun in my home, or heavy sedatives, I cannot predict what night of alcoholic madness might have led to my own death by suicide. I had already taken enough pills to kill myself as a teenager and probably survived by throwing up most of what could have done the job. Most people in the professions that study suicide agree that medication for depression and suicidal leanings is not the only solution, but must be combined with therapy and self-examination, along with, in many cases, a total change of attitude.

> Tell your children the true story. Do not lie.

But if we have personal tendencies to depression, and to suicide, we must, as suicide survivors, prevent the suicide of our own lives by not listening to the darkness, and instead turning toward the light. We must break the secrets, we must get the right help, find the right support.

We must tell the truth.

END THE CYCLE OF PAIN

The same energies that can doom you can delight you; and the same energies that can destroy you can lift you. Our job as survivors is to transform darkness into light. We know too much to leave others in the pain we must learn to survive. The more we can share our grief, tell the truth, and talk about the real facts of our beloved ones' lives, the more chance others have of not repeating the pattern.

There are no "correct" ways to grieve, but there are certain truths; one of these is that for those of us who have lost a loved one to suicide, we have to be aware that we are in jeopardy of taking our own lives. Statistics tell us that. But now we know the pain that follows in the wake of a suicide, and we have lost the "choice" to take our own lives,

> I think that when the lies are told and forgot the truth will be there yet—It don't move about from place to place and it don't change from time to time. You can't corrupt it any more than you can salt salt.
>
> CORMAC MCCARTHY,
> *No Country for Old Men*

though we may ache to do so, we may feel nothing is left for us, we may cringe at the thought of going on with our lives. But we must.

When I feel that hopelessness about my son's death, I must share these feelings with someone else, or I will break apart holding them in and do things, not even realizing I am doing them, that may be destructive to my inner peace and happiness.

I have to break the spell, and talk about what I am going through. I have to talk about the shame, and the fear, and the demons that haunt me.

> I had to learn to accept the truth, that nothing I might have done could have prevented my son's death.

Our purpose as survivors is to not lose ourselves in the feelings of emotional bankruptcy, chaos, and pain that come with the loss. We have to learn how to combat the genetic paths, the depressions, and the sometimes preordained feelings that we, too, must follow that devastating path.

LOSS COVERED BY LIES

"We had to bury my father in unhallowed ground," I was told by the mother of one of my granddaughter's friends from school. We were talking of family history, and how different families handle tragedy, particularly that of a suicide in the family. "We got rid off all his photos, his journals, books, his clothes. He was lost to our family, because he had left our family shattered by his suicide, and no one talked about him, no one ever mentioned his name again."

I have heard this story many times. It is one of the stories that perpetuates the taboo of suicide and terrifies the survivors.

But it can also be part of the hidden truth in losses of another kind—the wish to hide the alcoholism that caused the son of a friend to be murdered in a bar fight while he was drunk; the family who wants a closed casket, and a closed discussion, about the mysterious death of a child. The darkness that surrounds sudden tragic loss can be difficult to handle for families, and often secrets and hidden truths cloud the family myths with questions that may never be answered.

Many people that I have spoken to have told me that now, after years of silence and denial, they have begun to talk about the hidden suicide, the covered-up tragedy—to tell the story, live out the pain, realize that there was no guilt, no shame, and no dishonor in the death of their

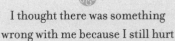

I thought there was something wrong with me because I still hurt twenty-eight years later.

LETTER FROM A SURVIVOR

father or brother or wife. These people have begun the important journey of retrieving the one they had loved and lost by telling the truth. They have stopped covering their loss with lies.

I received the following letter from a woman I will call Sandra.

Dear Judy,

My elder sister, Karen, committed suicide twenty-eight years ago. I did not have a support group to attend or a loving mate to help me. Instead, I really wasn't allowed to talk about it—I got the message that it was a family secret. There was no funeral for Karen, not even a memorial service. When Karen died, I was twenty and had just joined the Catholic Church. I went to the church office to arrange for a memorial Mass for her. The church secretary asked me, "How did she die?" When I told her, she said, "Don't tell Father, or he won't say the Mass for her."

On the morning of this "surreptitious" service, my car didn't work and there was nobody to take me (nobody else in the family was Catholic), so I didn't even get to attend that.

Today I'm married and have four children—ages thirteen, eleven, and seven. I never imagined what it would be like to tell them about the aunt they never knew, and it hurts. Yet it's also good, because I love Karen and my kids deserve to know about this cool young woman who was—and always will be—my big sister.

With affection and gratitude,
Sandra

I found this letter particularly moving, because in it Sandra shares her years of turmoil and fear—the "hurt" that some-

times expresses itself consciously, but is often buried beyond recognition, something that may cause illness, depression, and many other symptoms, even death—by one's own hand. Sandra was

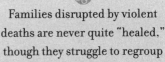

> Families disrupted by violent deaths are never quite "healed," though they struggle to regroup and redefine themselves in ways that might be called heroic.
>
> JOYCE CAROL OATES

fortunate that she felt the sadness and the hurt, because these are the touchstones of recovery.

It is also important for Sandra's children to know that their Aunt Karen's suicide is something they might want to pay attention to in their own lives, since studies show more and more evidence for genetic implications in the background characteristics of those who fantasize, attempt, or complete a suicidal act; alcoholism, depression, chemical imbalance, and many other predetermining factors are facts that need to be known and understood so that measures can be taken to ward off their possible effects.

> Tell the truth and walk through the fire.

The truth does not shine in vain. The truth breaks through the darkness. It brings out healing. It fosters joy and acceptance, and makes us grateful that we knew this person, and can celebrate his life, not only ache with loss for his manner of death.

It can take decades for the truth to come out, as it did for Sandra. If children in a family do not know the truth, and if they are lied to about the facts, they will often make up something more terrifying in its implications than what really happened.

> In the hands of God even the darkest path can be a great possession, for it can lead to the light of forgiveness and healing.

Truth lifts the cloud of uncertainty and clears the air. Truth: tell it, if it happened yesterday, if it happened thirty years ago.

Truth Affirmations

The Truth is my trusted servant and enlightened guide.

I will tell the Truth and let it set me free.

As long as I am in the flow of the Truth, I am safe.

My fears of the Truth are only shadows that haunt me till I face them.

I will refuse to surrender to the fear of the Truth that may corrupt and injure in ways I cannot see.

My innermost guides will bring me safely through to the Truth.

TWO

Trust

Allow it. Don't let the painful circumstances
surrounding the death of your loved one keep
you from talking with friends about your loss.
Trust the people around you to give you the
support you need, and if they cannot, find people who can.

Trust Affirmations

I will Trust in my power and my energy, my light to get me through this terrible time.

I will search for a faith and Trust that works.

I will Trust in nature and the seasons, in the cycles of birth and rebirth.

I will Trust deeply in the organic health of my body and my mind to recover.

I will Trust those who have gone on the path before me and can guide me.

I will Trust with all my mind and heart and soul that what I cannot see can heal and help me.

In the fury of the moment I can see the Master's Hand
In every leaf that trembles, in every grain of sand.

BOB DYLAN, *"Every Grain of Sand"*

*I*n surviving catastrophic loss it is important to find things
in our lives that we can still trust in. It could be a friendship, a spiritual or religious practice, the talent we have for
gardening or for nurturing our children and our families.

My faith, my trust in the world, was shattered when I lost
my son. I had to rebuild it, moment by moment, breath by
breath. I shuddered with despair and my mind searched
everywhere for the trust that had been smashed into
smithereens. I looked to my friends, to my God, to my habits
of life. The slow rebuilding of that trust has taken every
ounce of my energy and my nerve. In the end, my trust has
been my foundation.

My son, Clark, celebrated his first day of sobriety on
Valentine's Day, 1984—seven years before his suicide; after

that Valentine's Day, and his subsequent sobriety, I was sure that nothing bad could ever happen to us again.

Most of the beliefs that mean something important to us we must take on trust; love and hope, anger and fear, imagination and instinct all happen without visible support. We yearn and weep, laugh and imagine, but we cannot touch these feelings. Our faith lets us believe that the sun will continue to come up; that there will be food on the table, sleep in the night, laughter in life; we trust that death, when it comes to others, will not destroy us. We trust in our intelligence, in our habits, in our ability to overcome difficulties.

I trust in God; God help my lack of trust.

> Who hath not learned,
> in hours of faith,
> The truth to flesh and
> senses unknown,
> That Life is ever lord of Death,
> And Love can never lose its own!
>
> JOHN GREENLEAF
> WHITTIER, "Snowbound"

I wake again to remember that you are gone and it is like a bolt of lightning through my heart. How can you be gone? Your child is in the world, beautiful and energetic; your cousins are here, so much like you in their humor; your father, your aunts, your uncles are here, how can you be gone?

And I am here, who would in the natural course of life, have been the first to go before you.

I had faith, but my faith was conditional. I had to relearn the faith of my childhood, the faith of my unconscious moments, the faith that lets me sleep at night, that keeps my

body breathing and healing and functioning. My new faith—
for it was new, made from terror, from desperation, from
knowing I could not live
without it—had to be based
on trusting that something,
some Power, would always
be there for me and that all
would be, was already, well.

> The worst that can happen
> already has happened.
> There is no more in life to fear.
>
> ADINA WROBLESKI

I have always believed, imperfectly but steadily, in God,
and in the ways of the spiritual path. I have searched all
through my life for that connection to the greater Heart, the
greater Good, from the years in childhood when I sang in the
choirs at church, lifted by the music. I knew there was more
to life than what we see and feel and hear. I have always
looked for God wherever He might be, in churches and in
fields, in melodies and in nature.

FAITH UNDER ALL CIRCUMSTANCES

I know that loss is part of God's plan
for us. Hard as it is to understand how
it should be so, anyone who has been
there will tell you that it is through loss
that they learned compassion, under-
standing, and acceptance. When my son died, I had to trust
that there were reasons, powers I could not see or be aware

> A faith that does not
> include every
> eventuality is not
> true faith.

of, that were being worked out. My job was to stay in touch with a guiding power through my meditations and in my heart even when I wanted to chastise Him, even when I wanted to deny Him, even when I questioned the path I found myself upon.

One of the things that I trusted was the process of keeping a journal, writing what happened to me, what I thought, what moved in my heart. After my son's death I began to put my thoughts into meditations to get me through the days, trusting that, at least when I was writing, I would continue to breathe and to think. One day during the first year after my son's death, I wrote in my journal, "My granddaughter is learning to dance. I bought her gold slippers and she is getting very tall. She seems to be healing, like a tall blond flower in a garden, growing in spite of her loss."

And I remembered an old friend writing after Clark's death that she imagined my son as an iris, "tall and slender, with those blue-violet eyes."

Conditional faith is not true faith.

I had begun to trust again in the joy of seeing a child who was of my flesh and blood grow into a beautiful young girl, a reminder of her father, yes, but a total person in her own right. I began to trust in her being and her ability to heal me as well.

The journal for that day goes on:

Time passes, slowly. The grief is different now and it does not break my heart so much to see the sun, to see a flower, to see the children, the birds singing in the rain, the light in the sky. At first in this terrible loss I would sit at the piano and weep as I played the melodies, and fresh wounds would appear when I saw friends who asked, "how are you?" "How I am" throbs through my body, this body I carry from one situation to another, trying to be a part of the living planet. I do not try to hide my tears. I am a long way from acceptance. But I hear my nephew play the violin, folk songs from a thousand years ago, and I can smile. There are not only thorns, there are roses. I know now that I will be able to return, and not, as I did in the beginning, fear flying off the edge of the world forever.

Roses where there are thorns, sun where there is shadow. Smiles where there are tears; hope where there is despair.

My trust was coming back to me.

MAKE TIME FOR FRIENDS

It was weeping in New York City. A gentle snow drifted over the bare branches of century-old trees and hovered over my beloved New York skyline. It softened the figures of cars coming slowly down Fifth Avenue, trying not to skid on the fast whitening street surfaces. The sky was crying, the city was bereaved, like the lament for Keats by Auden, like the songs the Irish sing that are poems for the world. All of New York shivered in my sorrow; the city wept in order to breathe, the weather was my inner weather. My heart hung on those bare branches, listing from the weight of the gathering snow.

I made my way from the taxi, high boots with pointed toes and narrow heels, taking chances on the ice that lay under soft cover. I had a date for coffee with an old friend, a woman who had lost her son years before. Her loss was, like mine, unexpected and tragic. I had not spoken all morning: reading the paper, meditating, writing in my journal. It had now been about a month since Clark's death and I was ten pounds lighter than I had ever been, skin and bones and shivering in my heavy coat. But I was cold from inside, not from the chilly weather.

Over coffee in the afternoon, in a safe place, the tea room of a Midtown hotel, I was crying over the scones, weeping into my coffee cup, trying to tell as much of the truth as I knew to Isabel, a tiny woman, blond and elegant. Isabel and I had been friends for many years and I knew she had come through difficulties as harrowing as mine. I wanted what my friend had—grace under pressure, valor amid difficulty.

Let me see a world today in which beauty still exists.

I had brought my journal, and I opened it on the table next to the pretty porcelain plate of scones. It was still so soon after losing Clark that I didn't see how the sleet could be falling, how the flowers on the plate could be there, so innocent, so certain of their right to be there; Isabel, sitting across from me so serenely. How could any of us be alive when he was dead?

I told her I was not certain any of this was real, for how could it be, how could the season be turning, when Clark was gone?

"Did you love him?" she asked me. I told her I had loved him beyond imagining. "And did he love you?" I said yes, that he had loved me, and that we had been friends, many of our old questions settled, and most of our past difficulties over.

"Then it is all right," she said, smiling and taking a sip of tea, a bite of a scone. In Isabel's company, my trust made a new, small step while the snow fell outside.

I had loved my son, sometimes desperately. He was special, lovable, kind, beautiful. At times I loved him more than I thought I could bear. I had wept with worry, with anxiety, in that love. The love was tangible, like a heavy load, like starlight, like the feel of fire in your heart, like smoke. Like heartache, like all pain lifting away at last. I had loved him like forever, unconditionally.

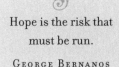
Hope is the risk that must be run.
GEORGE BERNANOS

Yet somewhere in the back of my mind I still wondered whether my love had been enough. I had loved my son, but

I suspected I had been less than a perfect mother at times. Yes, I always tried to do the right thing. But I was drinking from his early childhood to the time when he turned nineteen, a long time in which to subject him to many imperfect actions, to be a devoted mother but be a shambles at times, perhaps ill-advised, certainly irresponsible. The time I sent him away to boarding school when he was only twelve, when he had become impossible, using drugs, acting out at school and making trouble. I had had advice—there were therapists and friends who said he can't stay at home, he is a danger to himself and to you. Oh, it was a mature, adult decision. Many years in which the wrong answers to the right questions had to do, when there were no others.

> There is nothing so much like God in all the universe as silence.
>
> MEISTER ECKHART

"And then he went to that school, in Maryland," I said to Isabel, "and he went down a hill on a sled in the early snow, and ran into a car and nearly died. I had gone to the hospital in Hagerstown, and spent two weeks by his side, waiting for him to wake up, first, and then waiting for him to talk, to smile, to hug me, to tell me that he had seen the light, and made a decision to come back."

"To you," my friend said across the table. "He came back to you, to be with you." The light was settling quickly now, it was past five and the windows were turning dark with shimmering streaks of snowy sleet falling, barely visible through the lace curtains.

"Yes," I replied, "but then I sent him away again. The 'therapists' felt he needed to be somewhere away, with his 'peers,' not me."

(These therapists, who called themselves the Sullivanians, one or the other of whom I saw for fifteen years, had a strange set of beliefs. They advised their patients to drink in order to calm anxiety; they thought children were better off in groups, apart from their parents, and often advised people about their parenting roles—as documented in the *New York Times* in the years after I had left their practice. I must have been blind as well as drunk, but I stayed with them for years, and in some ways I benefited greatly from their unusual wisdom about creativity and being a successful artist. By other notions I was ill served. But I believe I had to follow something, and they were the people I chose to tell my story to. As it turned out, they knew absolutely nothing about alcoholism, which happened to be my true problem, as well as my son's.)

> What do you think has become
> of the young and old men?
> And what do you think has become
> of the women and children?
> They are alive and well somewhere;
> The smallest sprout shows
> there is really no death,
> And if ever there was it
> led forward life . . .
>
> WALT WHITMAN,
> *"Song of Myself"*

My son and I looked for the "right school" again, after he had healed from his head injuries and recovered in New York. A place emerged after a while, a cluster of odd-looking buildings in the woods near a small city in Vermont. He would keep out of trouble there, I thought.

> The greatest battle in our lives is to go on fighting against the demons of darkness and depression.

"We both agreed it was the one for him. And I sent him off again," I said to Isabel.

It was called Glenrock, a very sixties kind of free school, where the kids pretty much ran the farm. Clark loved it. He got into more trouble, of course, and was sent home quite a few times. But he seemed to get on very well, and I thought, well, this is going to be just fine.

"You know, people make their own luck," Isabel said.

I was barely a month past my son's death and this jour-

> I had to trust in God, in the process of friendship, and in the need for being alone.

ney out into the snow to meet with a dear friend was lending me some courage.

Make time for your friends as you embark on the grieving process—they will help you, they will carry you through.

I have a friend, Lorna Kelly, who became a devotee of Mother Teresa, and spent a number of years visiting the Sisters of Charity in Calcutta. There, she would work along with the sisters and talk with Mother.

Lorna was the first female auctioneer at Sotheby's in New York. Lorna is a stylish, beautiful woman who grew up in England and has had much success along with much travail in her life. She led a very high-powered and high-profile life in the big city, until one day in a sudden flash, she realized she had to go to try to help with Mother Teresa's work. Her book, *The Camel Knows the Way*, tells the story of her life and her relationship with Mother Teresa. Soon after Mother's death and the Beatification, Lorna sent me a wonderful video of the great Healer's life. I was moved deeply and taken by the sentiments, which I recognize as the testament to her work and to her life.

After Clark's death, Lorna was making a trip to visit Mother Teresa in Calcutta. She asked me for a photograph of Clark, which I gave her. When she next met her friend, Mother asked about Clark, about his life, and his death, and Lorna, who had known my son, told her all

> God's love is infinite, full of tenderness, full of forgiveness, kindness and thoughtfulness. Doesn't matter color, it doesn't matter race, it doesn't matter nationality, it doesn't matter religion; Hindu, Muslim, Buddhist, Jew, Communist, Christian. Every single man, woman and child is the child of God, created in the image of God, created by the same loving God. We are brothers and sisters.
>
> MOTHER TERESA

about him and gave her Clark's photograph. Mother Teresa put Clark's photograph into the back of the Bible she always carried with her, saying she would pray for him. And for me.

> God is Life, Truth, Love, Intelligence, Soul, Spirit, Principle. God has every quality of personality except limitation.
>
> Emmet Fox, *Around the Year with Emmet Fox*

This loving gesture gave me such comfort. What if each of us were to make a gesture like that, say, once a month, toward a stranger whose face we'd never seen? I like to think that the world would slowly shift away from the dark and toward the light.

KEEP TRUSTING

I believe in the Power of Great Force—God, if you will—that travels through all our vehicles, our religions. The practice of faith must be part of my life in order for me to thrive, to love, to be positive, to change my attitude when it needs changing. I believe that God, as I understand Him or Her, can do anything and everything that I might need in my life. My faith was not destroyed by tragedy; on the contrary, it was deepened, and strengthened, and enforced by the catastrophic loss of my son. I had nowhere to go but deeper; deeper into meditation, deeper into healing, deeper into a quiet that would lead me to my own center, and let me sit in contemplation of the Great Being, for me, the force of the Universe, whom I choose to call God.

To continue to live, I must continue to trust. In my heart of hearts, I think that if my trust goes, my whole body and soul will evaporate. I will not be able to survive if I cannot trust. Those tender moments of love that came to me from my earliest memories—my mother holding me, my father's bright vision though he could not see me, his trust that I could succeed at anything, though my courage had not been tested. The trust that my family would make it through good times and bad, the trust that people were fundamentally good inside—human beings fraught with troubles but fundamentally good intentioned—these deep trusts had brought me through seriously difficult things in life. If I could not trust, I knew I would not make it.

Though I am not a Catholic, I have been affected deeply by many inspiring Catholics, from the Berrigan brothers (whom I visited in jail in Danbury,

> We trust infinite God rather than our finite selves. . . . Just to the extent that we do as we think He would have us, and humbly rely on Him, does He enable us to match calamity with serenity.
>
> BILL WILSON, *Big Book of Alcoholics Anonymous*

where they were incarcerated for their antiwar stance in the sixties) and Thomas Merton, whose life was an ode to beauty and poetry, and silent prayer, and who lived in the monastery at Gethsemane near Louisville, Kentucky. I ran across a quote of Merton's recently in his book *The Intimate Merton*: "Suddenly there is a point where religion becomes laughable. Then you decide that you are nevertheless religious."

I love Merton! He is so damned human! And, of course, religion sometimes is a false structure that prevents spirituality from entering. It was never so for Merton; hence his beautiful vulnerability and questioning heart, riveted to faith, while questioning structure.

Sister Maurice, a Catholic nun who has been in the Cistercian order for over fifty years, says that when a person dies, that means his or her work here is done.

But what is my work now that my son is gone? In the years since Clark's death my own story has changed so vividly that there are times when I do not recognize my former self. Yet I have come to see my son as a teacher and his suicide as a mission that was begun before he was born, and lives on after his death. The work, as I know it, as I do it, is about his legacy, which is love, and light.

And then a sudden darkness that enfolds me. There are only slight intimations of where I am supposed to go.

Many times since I lost my son I have sat meditating in the room in which I now sit. In the year after his death it was a different room; there was very little in it, it was painted white, and I had just taken it as a sleeping room and studio, so there was just the bed, a few books, and a table or two. One afternoon I sat on the floor meditating, a candle burning in front of me, the tears falling down my face. The room itself was also filled with a powerful roar of horror. I could not believe there had not been some mistake, that my son had perhaps been murdered or I had misunderstood, he must be alive, not dead, there on that bier in the mortuary. My mouth fell open and I wept and screamed at the sorrow in it.

I am beyond reasons, there is nothing I can figure out. I have done the writing and the crying and the praying, now I have to ask God to help me live through your death. I must trust.

ANONYMOUS

It was just a few weeks after I had kissed Clark's face for the last time, just before they rolled him into the fire. I had been given his clothes, and they smelled like smoke, like the carbon monoxide that killed him. It was spring, and I looked out the window onto the air conditioner and saw that the egg of a dove had fallen, and broken there, its yoke mean and desecrated, and I saw the mother flying off, no more egg on which to sit, no little dove to fly from her nest. For the rest of the day, and even now, years later, I could see that broken egg and that abandoned mother. But I am still here, I must tell myself, and you must tell yourself, too. I am still here and I must continue to work, to find purpose.

TRUST OTHERS WITH YOUR STORY

The telling of my own story is the telling of all stories, for in telling the personal, the heartbreak, the details, is the universal. I have to trust you with my story, and hear your story with ears wholly bent on listening, on not judging, on truly hearing.

A few years ago, after writing *Sanity & Grace,* I had become an occasional speaker at conferences and suicide prevention groups, and for that purpose, I went to Chapel Hill, North Carolina, to speak at a luncheon to raise money for the local Suicide Prevention Society. It was spring there in the South, early and rich with the smells of loam and wildflowers, and it came just in time for me. I had been stomping around in the snow in New York or out on the road in freezing rain and sleet for months, it seemed, and the sight of the tulip trees, and the soft greens that come up in the Smoky Mountains around Chapel Hill moved me, refreshed me, and made me feel that I, too, would bloom again, and grow again, and keep on healing.

It was early April, and thirteen years, then, since my son's death. All I had to speak about was my journey, whose

> Become yourself. Seek God. No less potent steps than these will be deep enough to move you forward.
>
> MARIANNE WILLIAMSON, *Woman's Worth*

only truly unique aspect was that it was my story. We all have stories, and each of us comes through with different truths.

THE DEAD ARE NOT GONE;
THEY LIVE IN OUR HEARTS

I hear Clark's voice when I am with my family. When we are gathered around a table I think that at any moment he'll enter the room and quietly join us. When my granddaughter is laughing, or my sister is making a chicken with the mushrooms he used to search for in the woods, I feel he is there. Whitman said it in "Leaves of Grass":

Failing to fetch me at first, keep encouraged;
Missing me one place, search another;
I stop somewhere, waiting for you.

When first reading this, I think, "How did Whitman know that?" Of course, he was human, but then, also, he served as a nurse during the Civil War. He must have seen terrible things, experienced terrible personal losses. He tended to one of his brothers for quite some time at the end of the brother's life. He knew of the price of life, the pain of loss. And without loss, there is no depth to joy, no plumbing the heights of life.

Clark seemed very present at the event in Chapel Hill, and I couldn't help pondering his beauty, his recovery from alcoholism, his bright laughter.

TRUST IN YOUR STORY

The people who ran the event could not have been kinder. In my room there was a basket of fruit and a keyboard, since they knew I need to practice when I am traveling. There were extra towels and extra feather pillows; the suite was comfortable and looked out into the blossoming tulip trees, where the birds were singing up a storm.

A number of people in the audience that noon were suicide survivors. Many of them worked in treatment centers for alcoholism and drug addiction, where the incidence of suicide and violent death is always present. Lunch was lovely, although I was not paying attention to the food, for there were stories of people who had come through great difficulties and were thriving, healthy, not depressed anymore in the way they had been; there were survivors who had been able to turn their experi-

> Religion is for those who are afraid of going to Hell;
> Spirituality is for those who have already been there.
>
> ANONYMOUS

ences to help others, and lead lives that were full of grace and service.

Chapel Hill is a community of tradition, where writing and storytelling are important to people. During our lunch, Helen, an African-American woman—shining, healthy, beautiful, about thirty—spoke from the podium telling a story it was hard to believe; the depths of her depression and degradation had been so severe. She had tried suicide a dozen times, run from treatment, sought her drugs of choice and relapsed again and again, and finally, after her last suicide attempt, found her way to a treatment facility where she was able to admit she had a problem, start to listen instead of "talking her trash," she said, and get sober and clean. She was celebrating five years of her new life.

> And death shall have no dominion.
>
> DYLAN THOMAS,
> *"And Death Shall Have No Dominion"*

"And the funny thing is, in these years since I have been sober, I have not been suicidal," she said as she finished. "Go figure!" The room burst into appreciative applause, and Helen stepped down, glorious, happy, and a powerful example to everyone in the room. I turned to the man sitting next to me, shaking my head over the power of what I had heard. He was smiling, and clapping, and very moved. There was a twinkle in his eye.

"It is amazing how she's gotten to a place where she can be so honest," I said.

"The story knows more than the storyteller," he said.

It is as though we are all swirling within the words and music of our story, and we tell each other about our lives so that we can better understand each other, and in that understanding of the other, understand ourselves.

Trust Affirmations

I will live my life in faith.

I will Trust that I do not have to hide.

I will go forward with my work, my friendships, my creativity, Trusting in the powers of the Universe.

I will find a way to Trust that I will be taken care of, I will be all right, finally; maybe even now.

I will let my fears subside and Trust in the greater power that guides me and all of us.

I will Trust that I can talk about the dark places, having faith that the light will come, as the dawn will come, in its time.

THREE

Therapy

Get it. Seek help, be it through traditional talk therapy, your art, meditation—whatever method you choose, or combination of those methods—but get the help you need. You must be your own advocate, and find the methods that will heal you.

Therapy Affirmations

I will reach out for help.

I will use spiritual as well as emotional networks to learn and to heal.

I will look for physical therapy, I will get a regular massage and have regular bodywork of some kind—yoga, Pilates, acupuncture, dance.

I will find a good talk therapist—someone who has experience with traumatic, sudden loss.

I will take an art class—painting and drawing can be a source of great comfort and healing in my life.

Laughter is therapeutic—I will put laughter into my life.

When my soul sees and experiences these wonderful things, my mood changes . . . I forget my sufferings and tribulations . . . as if from . . . a fountain, which always remains full and inexhaustible.

HILDEGARD OF BINGEN

TALK THERAPY

Life comes at us, we have to face it, in some way. And in every culture through the centuries there has been a recognition that we need more help from others at times that are difficult in our lives.

Use the therapy that is near you, and uncover other methods that can help you. The journey to find the right therapy—art, talk, body, mind, spirit—will go far to help you in your journey. Perhaps it will not speed your recovery, but only be a great companion of hope. That hope is going to help you.

Therapy made the difference between life and death for me. One particular experience helped me at a critical time in my recovery, when Louis, my wonderful, beloved husband, took me up to the woods of northern New York state to a spa where there was a fine therapist he had heard about, Deboroah Morris, and I talked and talked to her. She was wise and told me this was a great journey in which I would find great gifts, if I stayed connected to it and did not blank out or black out (or start using drugs and alcohol again—I was thirteen years sober when my son died). Deboroah helped me with her great talent and her great wisdom.

You must believe that you will recover, that you will smile, that you will thrive. You are here. You are alive, breathing, yearning, weeping. You are all the things that beat in your heart, that speak in your imagination; you are the singer, the writer. You are the mother, the daughter, the father; you are the son, the brother. You are a perfect being, you are a perfect person, simply grieving.

I had to believe I would recover from my son's death, I had to find the hoops that would bind me to life again. I needed to reach out my arms and my mind and my soul and let the feelings flow out, let the tears come. I needed to sleep round the clock and bask in the comfort of friends and strangers; I needed to find their voices and their caring in the darkness from which I did not want to emerge.

But the voices reach us; they say come back, we are here, you are alive and you will live another day, many other days. We can help you, lure you back to life.

LIVING IN THE SOLUTION

I went into therapy when I was twenty-three. I was depressed, living in New York, separated from my first husband, trying to get custody of my son, Clark, and knew that my drinking had something to do with the depression. I went to see a therapist because a friend told me that he knew someone who was seeing him, and had stopped drinking hard liquor and only drank beer. I had no idea that only drinking beer would not solve my problems, and I didn't curb my drinking at all during those years with this therapist, but I did start to talk—about my pain, about the suicide attempt I had made when I was fourteen and frustrated over not being perfect, about my dad's drinking, about my hurts, my son, my divorce. I talked, and talked and talked and talked, and that was something I had never done. I had performed, and succeeded, and knew how to work, but I didn't know how to talk, to communicate my pain.

In therapy with my first therapist, I began to learn that there was help. I believe that all my energy, my gifts, my ability to live and breathe have been given to me by the power I choose to call God. I believe in prayer. I had to pray for the health of my soul. And I believe there is nothing I can fake in building my own soul's experience. My life must have authenticity, it must have the resonance of truth, of life truly lived as I can understand it, in order to build my own soul's strength and purpose. I do not believe this is entirely an unconscious, nature-given gift. I believe that I have to work for it, learn for it, and help nature along. I must hear the drum of clarity, of meditation, of purpose in my thoughts and my actions. And I must follow that higher call, not listening to the baser desires and the lower pull, which is also always

You can only be halfway into the darkest forest; then you are coming out the other side.

CHINESE PROVERB

there to bind me in its spell. Sorrow, darkness, loss, negativity, depression, the yearning toward the blackness—I must fight them all the way, with every ounce of strength I have! Give me the light, the air, the purpose of God's will in my life. This is where meditation and prayer must lead me.

I started writing, getting the journals out and doing the work day by day, telling the tale, talking about my rage, my sorrow, my new kittens. The new kittens were such a comfort, purring and needing puddings and promising me that they loved me. The therapy of living, breathing animals who trust us with their lives helps us heal.

I went to museums, finally, and I went back to work, not canceling all my concerts, all my plans, as I had thought I would. I went back to talk to a therapist I had seen for many years after I had gotten sober. I saw him more than a few times, and went to see his wife, too, who he thought could be of even more comfort and professional help than he himself; she was a mother, she would understand.

It is important to find people you can reach out to. I have found that the therapy that happens among friends who share similar experiences is vital to our recovery. I spoke often to my friend, Jeanette Mason, who is a grief counselor, as well as a suicide survivor. Don, her partner, had gone out the window of their apartment the year before Clark's death, and there were times when I would call her every day just to get the courage to go on. Every conversation with someone who had already been down the path I was traveling seemed to help me.

> Where there is no meaning, both death and life can seem pointless, but where meaning can be discovered, perhaps even violence can be redeemed.
>
> JOYCE CAROL OATES

I went back out on the road, doing my concerts. It seemed impossible for me to even concede that this would help me, that working would be part of the therapy I needed. I could not think only on my loss; I had to think on, and work on, the things in life that gave me, and give me, pleasure.

Also, I had to make a living.

God, I believe, gave us work so that we can remain teachable. There is no education quite like working, doing the things that have been given to you, the talents you have been born with and work to improve, to hone. I have found that in my work is the stream of the river I have to travel in order to keep on learning and to keep on healing. Every day is a lesson, because every day my son is still gone, and every day my life must go on. Working is a tremendous therapy in that it takes my mind off my own difficulties, and puts me in relation to other people, people who have needs and moods and inclinations that I must adjust to, or go down thrashing in anger and in resentment. I have to adjust, and I have to keep being open to others, to their needs. This therapy is always there, unscheduled, unbilled for, and always in my path, for my life, and my work, involves other people. They save my sanity every day by being there, working with me, crying with me, sometimes fighting me.

Your work can be the most powerful of therapies. If you don't have work you love, find something you love to do; volunteer somewhere so that you will hear other stories, meet other people whose sorrow is maybe greater than yours, so that you can see we are on this path together and have to help each other as best we can.

I painted, doing watercolors that gave me some light in the dark. I read books about loss, and about healing.

I got physical therapy, massage—sometimes every day in the first year. The massage helped me get back into my body and out of my grieving head. My heart responded, my skin and my eyes. I looked at paintings, I went for walks, and nature began to be my therapy again.

MEDITATION IS INSTANT THERAPY

Many people, and I include myself, have found that meditation can do what drugs, and many other forms of escape, cannot accomplish—it can calm you down naturally, and put you on the right track without a prescription. It is the first line of therapy, the kind that is free. Turn off the phone, sit in the quiet, light a candle, say your thanks to whomever you thank, count your breaths, list your loved ones and friends and gifts, be grateful to God, and you are there.

I started meditating when I was in my twenties, following the gurus of the times. I was in a private audience at the Plaza (yes!) to hear the Maharishi speak, and read Krishnamurti. I went to yoga classes on the Upper West Side of New York; I was still drinking but I found solace and peace in these times, and I knew in my heart that I had to find a way into a steady and regular practice of meditation.

Except for the music and the prayer, meditation had not been a part of my religious education. They say that religion often stands in the way of the religious experience. Eventually, in my early forties, after many years of searching, I found my practice, which is called SRF, Self-Realization Fellowship. There are all kinds of meditation, and this one, begun by Yogananda, the first Indian guru to come to the States to start a school (in Los Angeles), fits me like a glove.

There are many kinds of meditation in many religions,

many practices you can choose from. You may have to try many forms until you find the one that suits you, from Zen to Western forms, but if you search you cannot help but succeed.

> When you become you, Zen becomes Zen. When you are you, you see things as they are, and you become one with your surroundings.
>
> SHUNRYU SUZUKI

Meditation was my first line of defense, and it saved my life when my son died. Clark came to me in meditation a few days after his death, and hovered in the candlelight near me with the most powerful resonance. He said, quite clearly, "Be careful, Mom." I was frightened at first, but then grateful to have seen him and heard him. They say that when a departing soul is passing into another sphere, sometimes that soul will pause on its way along that path, to give comfort, to give warning, to give some signal, some explanation. Some hope. What was my son saying to me about his life, and about mine? I felt the danger my son warned me of. What impact was his suicide having on my soul?

I think now, after having gone through this terrible darkness, that the tragedy of losing my son had threatened to shut my soul down, to end my search, and to silence me. In the silence of my meditation, Clark wanted me to see this potential. My soul had come to the razor's edge. At this time I had no way of knowing whether I would succumb to the dark, smoldering silence that hides behind the hand of tragedy, but now I know that there is another kind of silence where I can find the peace and purpose. Through meditation, I found this silence.

HEALING THERAPY

Before September 11, 2001, I had not had much experience with the great community of firefighters in my city. Nearly three thousand people were lost in the attack on the Twin Towers in New York, 343 of them firefighters from the New York area. The tragedy of this loss has not only changed the world but has also touched people everywhere. In the aftermath of 9/11, I had the honor of meeting many of the heroic firemen and women who had become survivors of the unimaginable. When I was invited to join the men and women at a handful of firehouses around New York for some talk and singing I discovered firsthand why firehouses are famous for their food. On several occasions I found myself with a lifted fork full of delicious pasta as the fire bell rang and the firefighters began to shove their feet into those ever-present boots that stand under suspenders and overalls empty and waiting beside the fire trucks. In my memories, the trucks

You are deep in the woods, and you think you are lost; stop, look at the trees, the rocks, rivers— they are not lost. They are here. You are not lost, you are here.

FROM AN OLD
AMERICAN INDIAN STORY

stand like shining, pulsing red and white teams of fire-breathing horses, fit and ready to roll. And over the firehouse,

Of course it is a struggle; out of rock, then out of mud, then out of heavy liquid, then water, then air, then light—then more light, then thought, and here we are . . .

FROM, *Letters of a Scattered Brotherhood,* EDITED BY MARY STRONG

deserted for the moment but for us visitors, hangs an eerie silence, the quiet of a house where courage lives and breathes, waiting for the safe return of its inhabitants, its legendary men and women of fire and smoke, of rescue and valor. I always found those firehouses, the homes of the bravest, holy places.

Captain Jim McGrath is a firefighter whom I have had the privilege of getting to know since the days after 9/11. I went out to his firehouse in Brooklyn where he was the Battalion Chief. Jim and I liked each other immediately, and over the years we have gotten to know each other a little. He has come out to concerts, and I have met his wife, Yvonne, his son Bill, and many of his fellow firefighters. I admire and respect Jim, and we have often talked about what it took to live through our losses.

Jim is sixty-two. He served two tours in Vietnam and then left the service to join Engine 256, the Dekalb firehouse, in Brooklyn, where he stayed for five years. He married Yvonne in 1974 and their son Bill runs the Jacques Marchais Museum of Tibetan Art in Staten Island, the largest Buddhist museum in the country.

Therapy

In 1975, Jim joined the Happy Hookers–Engine 279, Ladder 131, and after a few years became Battalion Chief of the whole Red Hook area of Brooklyn. He was Battalion Chief on September 11, 2001, when the Twin Towers went down.

Jim was at home that day, having a rare day off. Yvonne called him in the morning to tell him that the towers had been hit. Jim put on his uniform, then headed to the headquarters of OEM, the Office of Emergency Management, and then went to Ground Zero.

> No rain,
> no rainbows.
> MADELAINE H.

Those days were a nightmare for all the men we came to call "the Guys." In the aftermath of the disaster, Jim McGrath would be there, to witness and to mourn, and to help out in any way he could. He said it was like a snowfall, part of it was so quiet, nothing but the slowly falling ash. (One of the things he was able to do in the area of the fallen towers, where hundreds of search and rescue workers were on call day and night, was to bring down the portable toilets—since there was no running water at all and services were at a minimum, it was a much-appreciated effort on his part. "Somebody had to do it," he said.)

He didn't make it home for three days.

Jim was part of the team that began to put together who was missing, and he would learn that among the dead that day he could number sixty-three men he knew by name. There were twenty men in Jim's battalion who died—seven from Engine 202, Ladder 101 (a sign on that firehouse says "Seven in Heaven").

In the old days, Jim said, a guy who had lost a man or been through a bad fire would pack up after the truck and ladder were back in the firehouse and go across the street for a few stiff drinks. That was their therapy. After 9/11, there was a therapist assigned to each firehouse in the city and the fire department learned a lot about the importance of therapy to the men and women who had lost their colleagues in this tragic manner. (The New York Fire Department formed in 1860. Since its inception, the department has lost a total of 1,100 people, that is, over 146 years—343 of those deaths were on 9/11.)

Jim told me, "I went down to my firehouse a few days after the Trade Towers went down, and there was this guy, in a suit, Warren Spielberg, and we started to talk, and soon all the guys were sitting around in this round robin, talking. And I was there, a sort of peer counselor, because I had had a lot of experience. I had been involved with what we called Critical Incident Therapy, which was started after the fire at the Happy Land Social Club—they provided training to fifty firefighters to do peer counseling in the aftermath of these things—we called the burns 'roasts,' just to keep them impersonal, you know. You get a cup of coffee, a bite to eat, and you talk, and anybody not sleeping became a coworker in the therapy sessions!

"And I had this puppet, like a little poodle or something, and I had dressed him in a fire suit, I took him down to the firehouse and set him up and did a lot of humor with this puppet dog, and they just howled, they couldn't get over it, they said we have to get help for this dog! It helps to laugh, and it helps to sit and listen, and then, there is the laughter, we get into that, and that is healing, too. It's like, we have to do that, we firefighters, or lose our way. We have to see the big picture. In my battalion and everywhere I went I heard the stories, every single man and woman spoke to a therapist, whether for an hour or for a few minutes; whether in groups or one-on-one. Everybody who could get it got help."

Jim was a safety chief, and as such did many of the interviews with the men, letting them talk about where they were, what they saw. A lot of this was done to find out what actually happened, and one guy would say "I was there" and "I heard that," and then we could piece together what happened. "There were a lot of us doing these interviews, and a lot of them wound up in the *Times,* you know. A lot of guys would leave the tape recorder on when the talk got

It's ironic, but until you can free those final monsters within the jungle of yourself, your life, your soul is up for grabs.

RONA BARRETT,
Miss Rona: An Autobiography

Most of us have had to live through the dark part of our lives, the time of failure, the nighttime of our lives. . . . The night of the past is gone, this day is ours.

HAZELDEN MEDITATIONS,
Twenty-Four Hours a Day

personal, emotional, you know. I would turn it off, and let the guy talk.

"The therapists had to tell us that it wasn't just personal for us, all this terrible loss. It was our families, too, who were suffering, and they needed therapy. Yvonne got therapy, too."

LAUGHTER, THE NECTAR OF THE GODS— THE BEST THERAPY

"There was one wake," Jim continued, "after old Gus McGinty was buried; Gus was an old-timer, he must have been about eighty, and he had lost his wife and retired from the force years ago, but he was always invited to the funerals of the men and women he had served with. There were masses of people at this wake, and his best

> Mutual forgiveness of each vice,
> Such are the Gates of Paradise.
>
> WILLIAM BLAKE, *For the Sexes:*
> *The Gates of Paradise*

friend, old Gerry Douglas, he had a lot to drink, and had cried for a long time and then laughed for a long time, and as he was leaving, or being helped out the door, as it were, he said, 'I haven't had such a good time since my wife died!'"

And when he told me this I remembered that, of course, it was the laughter that finally began to plumb the depths of my grief and allow me to come up for air. Laughter, pure gold—laughter, nectar of the Gods.

ART IS THERAPY—SEEING IT, MAKING IT

I always have had to talk through my feelings, even when I was little. Music helps me to verbalize my response to beauty, and the fear and the awe and the sorrow of death. Through my music I speak what is on my mind.

What kinds of activities can I put into my life that would stimulate my creativity and help heal my loss (painting, singing, writing, reading, a new sport, a trip to the museum)?

We feel things more deeply when great art is nearby; it allows us to understand that we are not alone, that people have been experiencing joy and sorrow of the deepest kind since time began.

I was in Bosnia and Croatia during and after the 1990 war in those countries as a UNICEF representative for the arts. UNICEF had designed a wonderful program for children in war zones. The

> In all true art, there is no expiration date. Words and music born out of the artist's pain, become an immortal and timeless Anthem for the reader. The great gift and healing of art is this harmonic connection with our collective grief, words WE would have written if we could summon them. The perfect words. This is the healing of art. As if to say, "You are not alone. I have gone before you and I have felt your pain and I have survived." This is the legacy between the lines. Hope.
>
> SANDI BACHOM, *Denial Is Not a River in Egypt*

children made paintings, and then drew for seven days. In the beginning, their drawings were full of the fires of war, planes dropping bombs, refugees fleeing, houses on fire, trees and children being blown apart. In the days that followed, they worked through the images in their minds, none of which included themselves. At last, after a few days of the drawing classes (held in hospitals, refugee camps, family compounds), the children would begin, tentatively at first, to draw themselves—a boy or girl standing in a field surrounded by flowers, standing in the sun, face beaming— arms outstretched, no sign of the flames and the bombs, after a while. Just a child, open, free, alive.

> Without absolute death, there is no creation.
>
> KRISHNAMURTI

To get to the painting of themselves, happy, joyous, child-like, the children had to draw the bombs and the terror.

Before we can begin to recover, we have to tell it like it is, or paint it like it is, or sing it like it is, or write it like it is. Or all of the above! To someone we trust. Art helps us trust that we can recover.

> Music and art will bring out the you in you; that is what they are for.

Henri Matisse, the painter who lives in our museums and our civilization and consciousness as one of the greatest artists ever born, was raised in much hard work, discipline, physical illness, and difficulty. He said of himself that he would never have been a painter if he not been unhappy. His experience of dissatisfaction fueled his extraordinary creativity. "You have to be sitting on a volcano," he said.

Of course, not all of us will find a volcano that can turn us into a Matisse; not all of us can become internationally known painters out of our pain, but that isn't the point. We know that pain is often the touchstone of beauty. We come from pain, and it guides us into desire and appreciation of the world in ways that we cannot apprehend until and unless we have experienced loss.

In the early days afer Clark's death, I found that if I could sit down at the piano for an hour a day, even when I found there were tears on the keys, the clouds would clear, my mind would recover a little, and I could get through that hour.

TALK THERAPY

A few days after the hurricane that swept the Gulf Coast in 2005, my friend Alicia Hetherington, who helped me so much when I was letting go of whiskey, called me to tell me she was alive. I had been trying to reach her and was thankful to hear her voice. Alicia has worked in casinos all her life and had moved to Biloxi to be near the water and the sun. I saw her a couple of years ago when I sang at the Beau Rivage, which is now totally destroyed. She was happy, living a life of service and serenity. She called to say I couldn't reach her—no cell phone—but that she had been bussed before the hurricane from Biloxi to Tupelo, Mississippi, where she had a room, with nothing but a cot in it; more than some had, much more than others. Though she had used up another of her nine lives, she was well. I pray for my friend Alicia, and for everyone who has lived through anything like this terrible, unimaginable loss of life and home and place. And I ask myself, How can we survive these terrible journeys? Of fire and water, of pain and despair, of those moments when we really know we cannot go on and yet, somehow, must.

Talking about it can heal us, and it can keep the love of our lost one close to us, and remind us that there is healing in memory, in keeping the best dreams alive for our lost ones, but, more important, for ourselves and those who remain.

Find people you can talk to. You might look for a group that specializes in tragic loss or the circumstances for recovery from your particular loss. There are many groups and individuals; there are shamans, priests, or healers in every culture. The American Indians have sweat lodges to heal the emotions, the Baptists have singing and praying, the Holy Rollers have whooping and hollering, and teenagers have rock and roll. We are creatures of emotions,

The only way to escape from the abyss is to look at it, measure it, sound its depths and go down into it.

CESARE PAVESE, IN
The Savage God BY AL ALVAREZ

of hurt and helplessness at times and, as such, we need more help, more compassion, more caring, more touching. We need more healing, more talking and listening.

Do not be intimidated by those who think you should be "over it" by now, whenever now might be, sooner or later.

GRIEF AND ADDICTION

When we are emotionally fragile, we are especially susceptible to alcohol and other addictive substances. Be it drink or drugs, our hearts and minds call out for relief from the pain. Know this and guard yourself against it as you slowly navigate your way through the pain of your loss.

Sometimes the time of greatest loss is also the time of self-healing for other major illnesses. Alcoholism and drug addiction are illnesses, not moral issues. At these times, when the bottom falls out of the life of an alcoholic or addict, his or her sobriety may be sorely tested. It might also be the time when an active drug or alcohol user finds the strength and courage to get help for the illness.

In our family, we had a secret—our gifted, rambunctious, wonderfully brilliant, well-read, entertaining, and talented father was also an alcoholic. We were stymied by the changes in his personality when he drank, the shift that took him from the great person, the great father, and mentor, to the shape and actions of a stranger. Chuck was wonderful. And then, when this other person took over, we did not know that he was not bad, that he was ill.

Because of his alcoholism, my father was a difficult man. We talked about books, and about poetry, and about politics. But we didn't talk about *"it."*

Let me still trust that there are things that matter and can heal me.

The most important and obvious thing in the room.

My father was a deep-sea democrat, to the heart and bones. He was kind to people, to my mother, to me, to my brothers and sister. He was intelligent, an amazing entertainer, a lover of good food and good friends. He had a beautiful voice that was lyrical and popular; he had one of those hard-to-ignore stories: a blind boy raised on a farm in Idaho, who had found out how to get around the world without a dog or a cane, and had fabulous stories of his life in the menagerie, as he called it, with all the other "different" and handicapped kids, the deaf and the blind, the damaged and sometimes the broken. He had spirit, my father, and people admired him enormously.

We didn't know anything about alcoholism, but we learned about secrets. We were not going to talk about the drinking if our lives depended on it. We must not break the silence; we would cause ourselves pain. Our father might become the "other": we could never know who he was when he was drinking. He was someone else, a stranger, noisy, rude, and unpredictable, breaking open the liquor cabinet when my mother locked it in desperation to keep him from the Jim Beam.

I was afraid of my father, of his rage, of his grief, which was overwhelming when he drank. I could not talk about how terrified I was of my father and of the alcoholic moods that overtook him. My father was powerless over alcohol, I know now, and my heart goes out to him, a warrior in that terrible battle, which he fought alone and yet inflicted on all of us.

> It is normal to be angry, hurt, paralyzed with fear. The guilt comes from the feeling we could have prevented the tragedy.

The alcoholic appears to become mentally ill when he is drinking, doing things he would often never dream of doing, humiliating himself, and often hurting those he loves. U.S. Surgeon General Vice Admiral Richard H. Carmona put together a list of facts about the disease of alcoholism and its effects on us and on our communities.* He says alcohol and substance abuse cost the American economy hundreds of billions of dollars each year in lost productivity, health care expenditures, and other costs; there are more deaths and disabilities (including suicide) each year in the United States from substance abuse than from any other cause; an estimated eighteen million

---

*Carmona, Richard H. "Prevention and Treatment of Alcohol Abuse: Vision and Strategies," from the National Medical Leaders Meeting held on February 12, 2004. You can find this on the Web at http://www.surgeongeneral.gov/news/speeches/alcohol_02122004.htm.

Americans have alcohol problems; five to six million Americans have drug problems; and more than half of all adults have a family history of alcoholism or problem drinking.

Carmona goes on to say, "One quarter of all emergency room admissions, one third of all suicides, and more than one half of all homicides and incidents of domestic violence are alcohol related." Before we knew that, in our family, we knew that.

> Whenever treatment directly neglects the experience as such and hastens to reduce or overcome it, something is being done against the soul. Experience is the soul's one and only nourishment.
>
> JAMES HILLMAN,
> *Suicide and the Soul*

Whether alcohol led to the loss of your loved one or it is exerting a powerful pull on you now as you grieve your loss, seek to understand that alcoholism is a disease and get the help you need to steer clear of it.

I do not think I would be alive but for the kind and professional help I have received. It is hard to find a good therapist, and when you do you will find they are better than gold. I did not have success in therapy by treating only my alcoholism. I needed other groups, of which there are many, where people who have the same problem I have are gathered and can talk together about it in a safe environment.

I have learned that talking to a therapist who does not understand the illness of addiction is a waste of my money and his or her time. And my time! One can find groups of like-minded people who are trying to stop using drugs or alcohol; one can find groups for all the losses I am talking about in this book. Like cures like, and the stories of others who have suffered what you have suffered can help you.

I have mined the territory pretty thoroughly and found a couple of truly great workers in the area of the mind—a rare few. They have helped me do more than stay alive; they have helped me thrive. I am truly grateful to them for listening, and, occasionally, talking.

I DON'T WANT TO LIVE IF YOU ARE GONE

I did go on; we do go on; we know we must go on. We have lost the choice not to, having seen the devastation that suicide brings. We could not bear to cause anyone else that pain.

EVERYTHING IS ALL RIGHT

I have a friend, Loretta Barrett, who likes to say that everything is all right. Not everything is *going to be all right,* but everything is all right. Now. This minute. In my heart. In the world. In the city. In my head. In my bones. Everything is just the way it is supposed to be at this moment.

I could not believe this, could not tolerate the thought; it made me sick, made me want to scream, to shout at the stars; this is not true, I wanted to say.

"The world is ruined for me. I cannot go on." Or, "I will not go on."

I know it is very hard for us to allow this thought. I found it almost unbearable, but somehow it helped me to surrender. To accept. To move on into the next moment, feeling each moment, as I went, sometimes even believing Loretta, that everything is fine.

I went to see the doctor I had talked to about life for thirteen years after getting sober in 1992. I was very angry with him because he had told me that I would not be able to stop my son from trying again to take his own life after the first attempt. I didn't want to believe that; I wanted to believe that there was something I could have done. This thought was useless. In spite of being angry that the doctor had said this to me, there was no one I trusted as much as I trusted him, and so in the weeks after Clark's death, I went to see him regularly.

One day I asked my doctor if I needed to be on medication, because I really didn't know if I was all right, if I was going through the motions, or feeling everything, or just in a make-believe place of my own making where I could get on with my life, and feeling feelings, but might be in danger of doing something unforgivable to my family. I did not want to go to the place I had been when I was younger, where I had tried to commit suicide.

We talked about this for a few sessions, my doctor and I. I got all the anxiety out, got out every thought and feeling about my own vulnerability to suicide that I harbored, and I came away agreeing with him that I was going through the experience of clarity. I had the meditation in my life, I had friends I was talking to, I had a good marriage. My husband was present, loving, available, and taking every step with me. I thought that was a miracle, but knew that it was one we had prepared for, in some way, during the years that preceded Clark's death. We had gone through a lot. We were, in some ways, as Sue Chance titled her memoir in which she described her own son's suicide, "stronger than death."

Stephen Levine, whose writing and philosophy have helped me to live a more spiritually oriented life, has published two books that particularly touched me and helped me survive, sometimes just the day I would read one of them. They are *Meetings at the Edge* and *Who Dies?* Both are filled with passages that stretched across the pages on certain

> We never fully come to grips with life until we are willing to wrestle with death . . . And the problem of death is posed most vividly in suicide.
>
> JAMES HILLMAN,
> *Suicide and the Soul*

days and grabbed my heart before it plummeted off the planet. He talks about the tremendous work it takes to go through grief:

She is gone now into her next perfect
evolutionary step, just as the unbearable
pain you feel propels you toward your next
stage of life and being.

There will be a pain following the loss of your loved one that will urge you to move forward in your life—to once again find purpose. But you will need help.

We must learn to find the help we need, the therapy, the understanding, and the compassion. When I began to emerge from the pain of my own loss, I remembered therapy had always been there for me, so I redoubled my efforts to find the right people to talk to, privately and in groups, who could help me go forward. I knew that through telling people who knew this road, professionally as well as personally, I could find healing. They could help my broken heart, my broken dreams, to heal. I also knew that my music and my writing would carry me through this time and that I had to force myself to embrace this part of myself once again. I urge you to find the therapy—or therapies— you need to survive the tragic loss you have experienced.

All training is preparation
to go beyond training.

STEPHEN LEVINE,
Meetings at the Edge

Therapy Affirmations

My light is shining and I am learning, healing, and going forward.

I have something to share with another, as I proceed on the path before me.

Part of my healing will be to tell others where I have been and what I have learned.

Therapy has begun to help me to find my own way, and tell my own story.

I can heal from this loss, for myself, and for my family, and my lost, beloved one.

FOUR

Treasure

Hold on. Don't stop treasuring your loved one.
Don't let the horrible events leading to his or
her death wash away all of the things that were
good and beautiful about that person's life. As
you let go, hold on, as well.

Treasure Affirmations

In remembering my loved one, I know I am celebrating her life as well as my own.

I will begin and keep a journal, to express my thoughts, feelings about the one I have lost.

If I am angry, I will try to remember anger is perfectly normal; I will not stay in the anger, but move on to appreciation of all the good.

I will record my dreams—especially those in which I meet again with my lost one. These nocturnal visits are powerful.

I will create a place of joy, celebration, and memory, a place in which I will remember and heal, that I will Treasure all the good things I can, so that I may be nourished, rather than demolished, by my loss.

And who will write love songs for you
when I am lord at last
and your body is some little highway shrine
that all my priests have passed.

LEONARD COHEN, *"Priests"*

REMEMBERING

It helps me to remember, as clearly as possible, who my son, Clark, was, who he looked like, what he sounded like. The memories of your loved one may be painful, terribly painful at first. But in the long run, they are going to help you recover, rejuvenate your inner life, and take you to the new place that now beckons in the aftermath of tragedy. Treasure your memories; they are your friends. They will help to heal you.

Of course, when I remember clearly, I also ask the hardest question—how did my son lose his good sense, his good instincts, and take his own life? That is the mystery of suicide, and a question many of us ask over the days and years of recovery. But it is also a useless question after the initial facts are discovered, for it is like asking why someone gets cancer, or has a heart attack; why he was there when the bomb went off and was killed when so many others were not?

Regarding suicide, the questions are always there, but many of the reasons people want to take their lives are psychophysical, and, just as alcoholism is largely a result of chemistry, these instincts are often rooted in complicated genetic profiles that have very little to do with what we might have done, might have said, or not said.

Try to let go of these questions and treasure all that you know in your heart was good in your loved one's life before he or she was taken from you.

When the memories of a person who is taken from us in a tragic way are forgotten, or hidden, there is clinical evidence that what we do not process mentally or emotionally can seep into our blood and our bones, our very cells, gravely affecting our physical and psychological health.

> I love thee with the breath, smiles, tears, of all my life; and if God choose I shall but love thee better after death.
>
> ELIZABETH BARRETT BROWNING, *Sonnets from the Portuguese*

Don't let this happen. Talk to your friends, to your family, to yourself, if it helps. Talk to your pastor, to your preacher, to your neighbor. Talk to your family, tell the truth, and encourage them to talk about the loved one who is gone. Share your memories.

CREATING A PORTRAIT

There is a photograph of her, for instance,
Standing with her young son, Clark,
in Colorado, where she came from, just before they
climbed some Clark-sized mountain.
They were dressed in rope, and boots, and khaki,
Posed along the sloping trail, and of the mountaineers
They might have been in some more distant time
(mountaineers like you or me) just two,
Coincidentally, turn out to be the ones they are.

Richard Farina, from the liner notes of Judy Collins
Fifth Album

Dick Farina, who wrote this poem, was a friend of mine in the early sixties. He knew my son and captured him, and me, in his poem. I put it on the back of one of my albums, along with the photograph he describes of Clark and me in 1966. For me, Farina's poem captures a precious time in my life and my son's life.

In a way, as happens to many women who have children at a very early age (I was nineteen), my son and I almost grew up together, making the best of what we were given, which was everything, in some ways, and not a lot, in others; when all the world was new and all the dreams were possible. When I read Farina's poem it helps me grieve.

Try to create portraits of your loved one in your mind that will help you to heal. Speaking to others who loved the person who is gone is wonderfully soothing, and confirming. Sometimes when I talk about my son to our family and friends who knew him, his being is vivid in the room, his sense of humor, his posture (his posture!—we were always having to tell him to stand up, but he looked beautifully relaxed and it wouldn't have been him if he hadn't looked exactly like he did).

> Blessed are they that mourn, for they shall be comforted.
>
> Matthew 5:4

Or you might try writing or journaling as a means of savoring the beauty of your experiences and even sharing them with others, your own family, lovers, wives, husbands, and friends. Creating songs and telling stories has always saved me. When my son died I had to go back to basics, to start writing and telling the story in ways that could heal me, as well as others.

I wrote songs about Clark. I sang them. I wept, but I also healed.

THERE IS LIFE IN THE DETAILS

My son, Clark, was a vision, tall even then; he had red hair and a quick smile and loved to fish, and to sing, and to read.

He was born in Boulder, Colorado, in 1959, in a Seventh-Day Adventist hospital, where they didn't serve meat or caffeine.

Clark was his own bright and individual person, complicated as well as clear as day. There is no one I know who is like him, though his daughter looks like him, and has his sense of humor, and laughs at the same kinds of humor he liked. He never laughed at the expense of other people, and neither does his daughter. How I miss his smile, like sunlight; how I miss his silliness, his beauty, his big feet; I miss his deep laughter and his joy at playing the guitar for me, and for his daughter and wife and friends; I miss his intelligence, like quicksilver, slightly wacky in his take on the world, just off-center of the way other people see things; how I miss his humor, his enthusiasm for his family, his child, for his work, for computers, for music, for his friends, for the band he played in, for the comic strips of Erik Larsen; his red hair, his lanky walk; his kindness, to strangers, to friends; his love of his family, of his uncles, of his grandparents. Of his half-sister, Rosalind. I miss the joy he felt about living in Minnesota, his celebration of life in the winter there, his pleasure in thriving in the cold weather, wearing that furry hat that covered his ears, singing to his daughter, fixing a busted computer, a broken car, a broken toy; how he nursed a broken heart, and took on the tough job of going back to school; how he fought his disease of alcoholism and drug addiction and how he won, for a while. I miss his keen appreciation of poetry and *Green Eggs and Ham* and Hemingway; his love of reading. Of music. His voice on the telephone, his face in the window, his figure at the end of the ramp at the airport smiling and greeting me; his pleasure in living in a city where there was valet parking at the airport, where the sky was clear of pollution and the river, the Mississippi, was full of fish; how he loved the family he had made, the new kitchen he had installed—the marble countertop and the disposal and the dishwasher—how he loved driving the family car, the Subaru; I had helped him buy it, cosigned for it, gone to Minnesota to help him pick it out. It was the car he would kill himself in, while he recorded a tape of his dying words, a sort of suicide blues. He should have lived to set it to music.

He didn't know there was life after midnight.

Your loved one is alive in the details. Record them in your mind or on paper, wherever you can. It is through the treasuring of these small facts that we keep the people we have loved close to our hearts.

SIFTING THROUGH THE LIGHT AND THE DARK

The loss of my father, Chuck, was my first great loss and it was all the more painful for the sense of guilt that hovered around his death. My denial of his illness was so powerful that I missed seeing him once more before he died. I could not, and would not, believe he was in grave danger. I believed the doctors, who could not find anything really wrong with him (he died of an aneurysm and in the late sixties there was no way to detect an aneurysm, although for years I held a deep grudge against my father's doctors, feeling they should have known, should have done more for him in his painful last weeks than they were able to do—resentment! And blame! They can corrupt our healing).

In 1967, for the first time, I had enough money in the bank from my concerts and recordings that I gave my parents a gift they never would have given themselves—a two-week trip to Hawaii, all expenses paid. A vacation in the sun. I didn't own a fancy house or car; I rented an apartment in New York and spent most of my money on my work, traveling around the country, paying my agent and my managers, and on vacations to Colorado, where I went to ski, to hike, and to spend time with my son and my parents and siblings.

I saw my father for the last time in December of 1967. We took a trip to Winter Park, Christmas in the mountains, the most heavenly place, for me, on earth. Daddy had been in a deep depression for a couple of years. I had

> Beware of desperate steps. The darkest day (live till tomorrow) will have passed away.
>
> WILLIAM COWPER,
> *The Needless Alarm*

paid to have him see a therapist, who called me to say she would have to discontinue the sessions, since my father would not talk about his drinking.

Funny, I have known many therapists, gone to many. His doctor was one of the few I ever knew until very recently who would give up a patient because he or she would not talk about, nor stop, their drinking. I don't know whether to thank her or blame her. He was fifty-seven. We did not ever talk about the fact that alcohol is a depressant. I don't think I even knew that, and anyway, I, too, was still drinking and had a long way to go to sobriety. Ten years, give or take.

So they went to Hawaii in March of 1968, and there my father suffered severe pain in his abdomen and was hospitalized for a few days. After they came back from Hawaii, he was hospitalized again, and then sent home, still in pain. I had concerts in England. I called my father's doctor and asked him whether I should cancel my shows and come home. He said, "No. He is going to be fine. And you will be here in a couple of weeks. Go on and do your shows." Daddy was dead four days later, a day after I had landed in London and a day before my scheduled Albert Hall concert. My brother Denver was in London with me, and I cancelled the show and we got on a plane for Colorado and the funeral.

Look at what you've left,
Don't look at what you've lost.
DR. ROBERT SCHULLER

I'll see you again
Whenever spring breaks
through again.

NOËL COWARD,
"I'll See You Again"

My mother asked us not to wear black.

It took me a long time to heal after my father's death. I had written the song "My Father" about him three weeks before his death. He never heard it. I was planning on singing the song to him when I got home.

He was my best friend, my confidant. In spite of the drinking. The person, along with my mother, who had encouraged me, had made sure I knew he loved my work, let me know in every way he could that he believed in me. That person, whoever it is in your life, is like a foundation, a rock when all else is awash in questions. There was never any question in my mind that my father thought I could do anything I set my mind to. He was gone now, and I was on my own. I felt guilt, I felt his specialness would be lost for me forever.

> To release the past, we must be willing to forgive.
>
> LOUISE HAY,
> *You Can Heal Your Life*

It was all true. He was irreplaceable. No one ever came near his unique position in my life. But I had to move through the loss.

In my family, we keep the memory of my father in all his goodness and imperfection alive. We talk about him, we think about him, and write about him. We praise his qualities and laugh about his fallibility, not in a mean way, but in the most loving way. He is a kind of marker against which most men in and out of power fall far short. He was ethical; he was educated. He was brave, fighting his blindness; he was a leader, schooling his children in all he thought important, in politics and human purpose, in books and in conversation.

So we kept him alive, and always have. Even my stepfather, Robert, who was a Chuck fan, like everyone else in Denver, long before he married Chuck's widow, has a running dialogue about the Chuck Collins he knew. Keeping him alive in our conversation has rescued my father from the failure of memory, and given a portrait of him to his descendents who will never know him but always know of his gifts as well as his weaknesses, for these are aspects of his person as well that should not, cannot, be forgotten. My father's strong, willful, powerful love of life and conviction that one person can make a real difference in the world serve as a powerful inspiration for us and we never allow the darker sides of his life to extinguish this light.

> What is certain is that they all suffered beyond description, to the point where suffering has become a mental sickness. And, as we bow in homage to their gifts and to their bright memory, we should bow compassionately before their suffering.
>
> AL ALVAREZ, *The Savage God*

THE GIFT OF LIFE

Ed Shneidman is the founder of the American Suicide Prevention and Recovery program. He started the first suicide hotline in the country in 1949 in Los Angeles. Suicide was such a taboo at that time that he was advised by many to take the word *suicide* out of the name of the hotline!

Ed has written and taught about death for sixty years. He has now retired from UCLA, where he is Professor Emeritus of Thanatology, the study of dying. Ed feels that the study of death increases our understanding for, and appreciation of, life; that an awareness of the dark side gives us the light to deepen the experience of joy in our lives.

Every suicide is committed by a complicated human organism operating within (or against) a large number of explicit and internalized subtle social threads; the study of suicide is, willy-nilly, a multidisciplinary enterprise.

ED SHNEIDMAN

Ed and I have a friendship that I treasure. I probably would never have had the opportunity to get to know him if I had not experienced the worst in life. That is the conundrum that appears so often—out of a place of certain darkness and death there comes some mysterious light, and we use that light to help us recover our own. Often when we talk on the telephone or I visit him in person in his West Los Angeles

Now may every living thing, young or old, weak or strong, living near or far, known or unknown, living or departed or yet unborn, may every living thing be full of bliss.

THE BUDDHA

home, Ed and I will discuss our families and our interests, which often coincide.

Ed has four sons, all doctors, three medical doctors and a dentist. The dentist, Jonathan, who is in his fifties, has just been called back into service from the reserves, to go to Iraq. He is a highly decorated officer, but of course, like other officers in Iraq, he will dress in khaki to hide his insignia, which otherwise might be a target for a terrorist or a suicide bomber. Ed is, of course, concerned about his safety.

Although I talk to Ed about Clark, and he himself has made a career of the study of suicide notes, initially getting into the field of suicide study through the suicide notes of thousands of people, he does not wish to read my son's suicide note, which has been transcribed from the tape that Clark made in the car while he was dying. It is his decision; I would be glad for him to read it. But he feels it would not be wise. Perhaps he feels he is too close to me, and might come to conclusions that would not make him happy, or that would affect our friendship. I respect his feelings. And I never want to read my son's suicide note again, either. I know what it says. It will never change.

Parting is all we know
of heaven and
And all we need
of hell.

EMILY DICKINSON

Ed and I often talk about the "Psychache," his word, that encompasses so much of the definition of a suicidal mind. He says it is a condition that drugs may help, but only temporarily, and the only way he has encountered to really treat a person who is suffering from what he calls psychological pain, even if accompanied by other diagnosable conditions, is to get them into a regular and trusting therapy situation, where they can talk and share about life and what their fears and psychic pain are all about.

Of course, this can take time. Years, often. It took me many years in therapy to begin to be relieved of the pain of that first attempt on my own life. After Clark's death, there were many more years of work to be done. The work, in a way, may never be done. It can be ongoing; that is part of the pattern of some recoveries.

And also the law of England wisely and religiously considers, that no man hath the power to destroy life but by commission from God and the author of it; and as the suicide is guilty of a double offense; one spiritual, in invading the prerogative of the Almighty, and rushing into His immediate presence uncalled for; the other temporal, against the king, who has an interest in all his subjects, the law has therefore ranked this among the highest crimes, making it a peculiar species of felony, a felony committed on one's self.

Encyclopaedia Britannica, 1777

My friend Nancy Knox says, "Every instance of pain in my life is perfectly constructed for the growth I need at that moment."

What I adore about Ed Shneidman, and what has made us friends, is that although we are very different people and come to the experience of suicide from different perspectives (mine being totally subjective and influenced by my experience with alcoholism in myself and in my family, and alcohol's influence on my son's suicide; and Ed's position as teacher, counselor, and scholar, as well as one who has not suffered the loss of a family member or close friend to suicide), Ed has the imagination and verbal skills to amplify his experience with life, and with death, in a way that encompasses literature, history, and humor. He is a kind, and very brilliant, as well as reachable and funny human being. We can laugh together, and also cry.

> I postpone death by living, by suffering, by error, by risking, by giving, by losing.
>
> ANAÏS NIN,
> *Diary, March 1933*

When Ed talks about his studies of suicide notes, there is tenderness as well as scholarship; he sees humanity in all its complication and bravery, as well as in its troubles. He has seen the part of that last century that may have been the most violent. He has studied violent death, and yet he talks of his wife, Jeanne, though she is gone now for a number of years, with the tenderness of a lover, and the insight of a devoted husband. And he speaks of his patients, the ones we are allowed to speak of because there is no patient confidentiality, as they are deceased, as friends, as complete people.

> Death ends a life, but it does not end a relationship, which struggles on in the survivor's mind towards some resolution.
>
> FROM THE MOVIE
> *I Never Sang for My Father*

When I am talking to Ed I feel that he never talks down to me, that he would never talk down to one of his patients, but that he hears me as a complex, and, I hope, by now, treasured friend as he is to me. His gift to me is talking in the present tense about past sorrows, in the past tense about friends he has loved. His teacher, Harold Murray, a professor at Harvard, was a tremendous influence. I have the feeling that Harry was a star, bright and fast, and burning, and that Ed, his friend, the quiet one, was probably necessary for Harry in order for the older man's light to kindle into flame. These people,

> Help me, oh God, to use the sacred memory of my loved one as a noble spur to consecrate the living. May I perpetuate and transmit everything that was beautiful and lovely in his character.
>
> From the *Book of Remembrance* of the Hebrew Congregation of St. Thomas, Virgin Islands

his old mentor and teacher, and his beloved wife, Jeanne, along with the haunting figure of Melville's Ahab, obsessed with the white whale, and the story of that battle of life and death on the sea, are as real as his figure, sitting in the garden in the back of his home on Kingston in West Los Angeles. Inside are paintings and sketches and drawings and woodcuts of whales, and first editions of *Moby-Dick*, as well as the paintings his father did.

My husband, Louis, tells me that Ed, who is eighty-eight, is in love with me. And I do love this man's mind, his scholarship, his erudition, and his humaneness. I know that Ed's true love affair has been the study of death, much to the benefit of people whose lives have been touched by it in some way. With his gentle, quiet, inquisitive, brilliant mind and words, I am quite sure Ed has saved many from their own self-inflicted murder in the wake of their tragedy, be it suicide or

> And God shall wipe away all tears from their eyes; and there shall be no more death, neither sorrow, nor crying, neither shall there be any more pain.
>
> REVELATION 21:4

other catastrophic loss. He has certainly helped me live through many days I otherwise might not have made it through.

Shneidman is a guide, and a teacher. I hope that in the wake of your tragedy you will find people like Ed. They are the gifts that often come out of unacceptable loss.

Treasure Affirmations

I will Treasure the people who shine in my memory.

I will Treasure my own work and vision that are helping to move me from paralysis to action, from mourning to morning.

I will Treasure the little things; coffee or tea in the morning; a walk in the park; a call from a close friend; the river, shining in the moonlight, in the sun.

I will Treasure myself, walking in the sun, remembering, but going forward.

I will continue to remember that my past is my friend and I can learn from it.

FIVE

Treat

Take care of your body and mind with exercise, meditation, and other relaxation-producing activities. Reduce the stress in your life. There is much you can do in your own time for your own recovery.

Treat Affirmations

I will Treat the body as well as the mind.

I will wake smiling, and say a prayer of gratitude for my life today.

I will take a walk today, perhaps a swim or a hike.

I will enjoy nature.

If I don't have a pet, I will get one. Unconditional love from an animal can be most healing.

I will learn to meditate if I don't already know how.

I will find a good nutritionist and continue a healthy plan of eating.

Truly it is Life that shines forth in all things!
Vast, heavenly, of unthinkable form,
It shines forth . . .
It is further than the far, yet near at hand,
Set down in the secret place of the heart . . .
Not by sight is it grasped, not even by speech,
But by the peace of knowledge, one's nature
purified—
In that way, by meditating, one
does behold Him who is without form.

THE UPANISHADS

PHYSICAL, EMOTIONAL, AND SPIRITUAL HEALING

There is much you can do in your own time for your own re-covery. Though it is important to seek help when we need it, we also must become our own helpers and healers, our own trainers, our own inner guides. Taking what we can from the outer world, we also have to find the strength from within to survive the terrible assault that suicide and sudden tragic loss brings into our lives. We have to find the things that work for us, and do them with determination, for we are on a mission equal to any in civilization—we are in the process of saving ourselves from extermination by our own negativity, fear, terror, and depression. In this chapter, we will explore ways in which we can take the healing process into our own hands.

When my son died I knew that I had to take the meditation, the exercise, the body-mind search for serenity, to another level. For many years, I had been exercising, drawing on the natural chemistry of my body, enlisting the endorphins to help me heal. Meditation was there for me, as it had been for years; now I prayed as though praying for my life; I closed my eyes to the firmament and found the powers were there.

EASY DOES IT, BUT DO IT

Depression is often a response to low levels of serotonin in the body, as well as other chemical imbalances. A healthy physical life can actually alter these chemical imbalances. Exercise can raise serotonin levels in the body and improve your moods for the better.

To cure depression, Dr. Andrew Weil recommends a half hour of physical exercise seven days a week, and lots of broccoli! I follow Weil's advice about this and a lot of other things. I consider him one of our mental health gurus.

Some people "treat" their sadness with alcohol or drugs. Self-medicating is not the answer. Try not to use alcohol or drugs excessively.

BENEFIT TO MIND AND BODY

I urge you to seek the benefits to your mind and body from regular use of these oxygenating, rejuvenating, and serotonin-producing activities.

As a teenager, I had no idea of the benefits of exercise. Exercise came to me in my twenties, as I was trying not to smoke and not to drink too much.

I began to learn that exercise was one of the only ways I could ease the anxiety I felt almost all the time. Pills and alcohol worked at times, but the overall sense of well-being, even within difficult emotional times, would only come when I had put exercise into my life on a daily basis.

Although all of my siblings are great skiers, I only started to go skiing two weeks out of the year when I was in my twenties. I would go to Colorado and

> The hand that veils the future is the hand of God; He can bring order out of chaos, good out of evil and peace out of turmoil.
>
> HAZELDEN MEDITATIONS,
> *Twenty-Four Hours a Day*

hurl myself down the slopes, getting into shape while I adjusted to the altitude, winding up bruised and out of breath, but in two weeks I would be in great shape! The problem was to find something that would work at all times during the year, day to day, month to month, year to year.

I found the Royal Canadian Air Force exercises in the late

sixties; they helped me quit smoking. I had to quit smoking because I couldn't breathe well enough to do the Royal Canadian exercises! I went to a salon in New York and worked with Jenny Craig as often as I could, stretching and wrenching my body into awkward positions. A couple of years later I found the swimming pool, and for many years thereafter I swam every day, rain or shine. The aerobic movement, the link with the subconscious that swimming provides, was so important when I stopped drinking, and for years afterward, that I continued my swimming every day.

Yoga was helpful for quieting the body and mind, stretching, focusing, and becoming limber.

I did bodywork other than massage and different forms of exercise.

In my late twenties I struggled my way through my active alcoholism and my fears and phobias, trying to stay in shape physically and mentally and emotionally. I learned about Alexander Lowen and his extraordinary work on body-mind healing. His philosophy was that many of our neuroses and troubles are set into our bodies from early trauma, and that physical manipulation, combined with verbal therapy, could often release these sometimes ancient patterns of pain and holding that can cause back problems and many other physical symptoms.

In 1968 I located one of his disciples, Bill Walling, and worked with him for a year or so. He did very deep work, sometimes painful work, particularly on my jaw and neck and back. I can remember one very painful session when his hands were in my mouth and I was yelling, telling him to stop. When he did, much of the tension in that area of my body had lifted. I had been Rolfed a couple of times by one of the original therapists at Esalen in California; this type of deep bodywork was painful but very rewarding. I then found, through some friends, the great bodywork guru Ilana Rubenfeld, and for the next two decades worked with her. She did Alexander work at first, a physical therapy centered around the posture; then she developed her own variations on Feldenkrais, and now teaches her own method, called Rubenfeld Synergy.

> Grief must run to hardness, fury and cold calculation and unless victory is wrought from this pain, it will all seem senseless, stupid, debased.
>
> SUSAN GRIFFIN,
> *The Private Life of War*

As a singer I am the instrument, and the voice is really the whole body, not just the vocal cords. Ilana was the thru-line of outer and inner changes. She was with me before I got sober and after; before I became bulimic and after I became abstinent; before I was married to my husband Louis Nelson, and after; before my son died and after. She is a light of healing in my life and I am very grateful to her today.

Today I use every form of exercise I can. I make it easy,

so that I don't have to go to a gym to get the endorphins going. I have a treadmill at home (as well as a stationary bike). Fifty minutes to an hour on the treadmill, at an eleven-degree incline, walking at a point-3 speed, five or six days a week helps steady my mind and my emotions. It also has made the altitude in Colorado a breeze! I can ski the first day, and not be wrecked. I throw in a few days a month of the original Jane Fonda exercise routine, which I have memorized. (It is a good idea to memorize a routine, so that you don't have to depend on a video when you are out traveling, which I am always doing!) In a hotel room on the road I run around the room while I watch television after doing a concert or giving a keynote speech. I can usually get close to an hour in, running with very little strain on a carpeted floor. In the well-constructed hotels with soft carpets, I run in my bare feet, which disturbs no one and makes the exercise routine easy. If I can, I go to the weight room in the hotel and use the machines, but often in this hotel-to-plane-to-venue-to-hotel-to-plane life I lead much of the time, I have to do what is easy and simple.

> Life isn't about getting everything right.
>
> SUE CHANCE,
> *Stronger Than Death*

When I am exercising, the heart beats fast, the blood is running to all parts of the body, and the emotions are focused on what is going on in the now. On many days after my son's death, I had to run until I practically dropped; walk until I was exhausted; swim until I had swum out the anger, the hurt, the pain, the denial. Endorphins are part of the fight-or-flight system in the body. They give us energy and a change of mood. Many days, when I was so angry I was in tears, or unable even to think about moving, I would start a slow workout and find myself feeling hopeful by the time a half hour or forty-five minutes had gone by.

ANIMALS ARE ANGELS OF MERCY

And then there is my cat—who heals me every time her purring body cuddles up next to mine, looking into my eyes, telling me she loves me perfectly. A friend told me that her sister, who had lost her husband, couldn't sleep, was suffering from what doctors told her was a form of schizophrenia; she saw many doctors, took every pill they recommended, and was becoming more and more shut down, exhausted, and unable to cope. A nephew, on a visit, brought her a gift—a Burmese mountain dog. A puppy. Immediately her life changed. She started sleeping through the night, gave up her sleeping pills, and began to laugh again, to love that puppy and take care of her, and the puppy in turn nurtured her. Animals have magical powers of healing for us when we care for them.

SOME THINGS CAN'T BE CURED

Seek help, help yourself.

I would also like to take a moment to recognize that some things may not respond to the efforts at curing. All around us there are "tools" being peddled—in self-help sections of bookstores and on television. We readily incorporate all of this advice into our own— whether it be Dr. Phil, Oprah, or Joseph Campbell; we may do Jane Fonda's exercise tapes and buy diet books from Atkins and Adele Davis. We get running shoes and go to the gym for fitness, and listen to the latest information on cholesterol and heart attack, on diabetes and depression; we see cancer overcome by the likes of Lance Armstrong; we hear about movie stars and people of wealth and fame who have come back from treatment for alcoholism; we buy the tapes of Anthony Robbins and kick-box in front of our TV set. We go on diets of rice and water, fruit juice and nothing but watermelon. We are strivers, we Americans. Yet we watch death in the movies, in the coverage of wars around the world, and the one thing we do not learn is how to handle death when it comes to us.

> Some problems last a long time, some a short time, but always there is a solution, and always the solution is to turn from the outer to the inner.
>
> EMMET FOX, *Around the Year with Emmet Fox*

We want to cure everything, and we are right to want to do that; this desire has eliminated diseases and created wondrous lives for people in many parts of the world.

But some things cannot be cured; some things have to be endured. I want to endure, and to do so, I have to do everything I can to remove my instincts for suicide by every method of prevention I can think of, learn, and incorporate. This is serious business, saving our own lives from remorse and despair, and we are going to need all the help we can get.

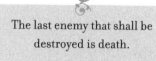

The last enemy that shall be destroyed is death.

I CORINTHIANS 15:26

A QUIET PLACE TO HEAL

When you are recovering from this terrible loss, there are lessons to be learned in silence, in contemplation. We cannot survive as thriving beings on the planet unless we feed the soul, and in recovering from traumatic loss, the soul is hungry for light, for company, for another solution, for tranquility in which to heal. You can go to the sea, where you are at peace, and be at one with nature. You can paint, being silent or absorbed in music as you do so. Music, by the way, can be a kind of living meditation, and there are beautiful tapes and CDs that can enhance your meditative and contemplative state.

SOME THINGS THAT HAVE HELPED ME,
IN NO PARTICULAR ORDER

At the age of eight or nine, I was already singing in the church and school choirs, and had been playing the piano for four or five years. I had been going to the Methodist church with my parents and my siblings every Sunday, and knew many of the hymns. But I thought something was missing. I needed a little more drama in my spiritual search, and so, following the lead of my Mexican neighbors for whom Mass, confession, and using the rosary were second nature, I decided I needed a "Holy" place in my closet in which I could communicate with Something, or Someone. Perhaps it would be the "God" Maria was always talking about. I set up a little altar, put a candle on it, and began to kneel before it at night until my mother found me and, in perfect Methodist manner, stripped my closet of the cross and the candle, and me of my hope to be forgiven, for what, I had no idea.

Meditation is the fundamental effort that exceeds all others, and transcends all other forms of healing. Meditation is different for everyone. For some it might be a walk in the park, for another going to a church, temple, mosque, or shrine. You may find that being out on the water, on a boat, is healing and contemplative. I like the meditative aspects of swimming and skiing.

But somewhere in my day—usually twice a day—I have

found that I must do some kind of formal meditation, be it a few minutes, twenty minutes, or longer. Finding that practice for yourself, in whatever mode you choose, will be uplifting and give you great inner power. The eyes upward, focusing on the breath, whether in Eastern or Western types of meditation, all seem to link us to the Universal Healer. Mingling and mixing the meditation with prayer will give you more choices—of gratitude, of resonance with those you love and even those who you do not love and may come to love. Forgiveness will evolve out of the practice, for we have to let go and forgive or we cannot be forgiven, and we must be forgiven. We are not perfect; we are moving toward our goals of comfort and a healed state. Consistency will be important for the maximum benefit from this practice.

> To practice death is to practice freedom. A man who has learned to die has unlearned how to be a slave.
>
> MONTAIGNE SOGYAL RINPOCHE, *The Tibetan Book of Living and Dying*

After Clark's death meditation came to me like a wondrous goblet of golden, sparkling, refreshing healing, the elixir of the soul, splendid and full of surprise. Clark would appear to me, speak to me, in the silence. I found the message that has no words, the sound of "Ommmmmm" from the universe. We might call it Kelven, the sound that oozes out from the multitudes of stars and galaxies, that is actually there, according to scientists, and reflects the Big

Bang or the hum of the sages and God himself, or Herself, perhaps. The silence is healing and holy and can come in the instant of watching a sunset, hearing the sounds of water, of birds, of music.

I like the silent morning and evening meditation, revolving around prayer. They dance together for me. There are many paths to meditation, such as the Maharishi's (on whose foot I put a red rose many years ago, and whose white robes and beautiful face I gazed upon for a few moments at an audience at the Plaza hotel in New York, not far behind the Beatles' path that had been beaten to the Maharishi's front door). I never knew what the Maharishi's particular method was, probably sitting, watching the breath, counting the breaths. I read much Krishnamurti and once went to see him speak at the New School in New York, and had an out-of-body experience while watching him with his white-clad, slender body sitting and talking. I did yoga sometimes, going to an Upper West Side New York apartment where Satchidananda's method was taught. The yoga relaxed and refreshed me, and my problems were lifted right out of my heart for the moment.

> The light that I see is not localized, but it is far brighter than a cloud which surrounds the sun—I call it the shadow of the living light.
>
> HILDEGARD OF BINGEN

I believe meditation is necessary to achieve calm and success, tranquility and peace, inner reflection and light. It is in meditation that we find our paths, learning that we already know the truth in our being, and opening our minds and hearts up to that truth. All other practices enhance the living, breathing, walking, sitting, silent, and noisy sound of meditation in your life.

LEARN FROM OTHERS WHO HAVE HEALED THEMSELVES

I was lucky to have found two sources of comfort when I was growing up in Denver—two people, in addition to my father and mother, who were tremendously influential in my life, and who, by their very presence, began to teach me about the power within myself to heal myself. I do not believe in coincidence. Or rather I believe coincidence is God's way of keeping His anonymity.

At the time, I didn't have any reason to suspect that these two individuals, odd as they were, unusual as they were, unique and different and products of the survival of great difficulties as they were, were each in their own way in possession of something magical, something powerful, that I would only later come to realize and appreciate, and practice for myself. These two people knew that one sure way to fully heal is to practice the presence of God in meditation.

The first of these two was my great teacher, Dr. Antonia

Brico, with whom I studied the piano from the age of nine to the age of fifteen. She was a dynamic, successful, and forceful woman, who struggled to do what to her peers was the impossible, and who also confided to me that in her life, at a particular time, she, too, had been deeply depressed.

> If you open yourself to loss, you are one with loss And you can accept it completely.
>
> *Tao Te Ching*

Early in her life, when Dr. Brico was living in San Francisco and going to Berkeley College in 1918, she was struck with the desire to become a conductor. She was studying music, excelling at the piano, but a passion to conduct held her, even though everyone she met, including world-famous conductors like Karl Muck, told her she was crazy even to think of such a thing.

> I'll tell you a great secret, my friend. Don't wait for the last judgment. It happens every day.
>
> ALBERT CAMUS, *La Chute*

"You can't do it," they said. "And why not?" she asked. "Because," they said, "you are a woman. Only men can conduct orchestras!"

But Dr. Brico kept the dream burning in her heart. Through the years at school in Berkeley, and then Juilliard in New York, she continued to study the piano, becoming a fine and accomplished musician. She continued to speak to everyone she met about her dream. They all told her to forget it.

In New York, where she had been admitted to Juilliard to

study piano and music theory as well as teaching, and where she practiced five or six hours a day at the Steinway showroom on 57th Street, she found her help, her healing, and her mentor.

Dr. Brico told me the story many years later. She said she began to feel she was losing her way, losing her commitment to her dream. She was even, she said, filled with the desire to end her life.

One night, as she passed Carnegie Hall on the way to her practice session at the

> Grief is like a wound. It must be kept clean and open so that infection does not set in.
>
> IRIS BOLTON, *My Son, My Son*

Steinway showroom, she saw the kind face of Yogananda, the great Indian yoga master and lecturer. His poster was fifteen feet tall and six feet wide, smiling out at her from the billboard outside Carnegie Hall. She and I were sitting at the old Russian Tea Room, a door down the street from Carnegie Hall, when she told me of her experience.

"I saw his face and knew I had found my salvation," she said, between spoonfuls of borscht and blinis with caviar. "I bought a ticket to hear Yogananda speak, and then I went backstage [Brico was not a shy flower by any means!] and became an instant devotee."

She also became a friend, traveling with the guru when she could. She told him of her great passion to conduct, and for once, someone said, "Of course, if you want to become a conductor, then you must do it!"

Yogananda arranged for some of his wealthier followers to support Dr. Brico's travels and studies in Germany. He encouraged her to audition for the world-famous Beyreuth music school, and she was accepted. By the end of her education there, she had become a guest conductor of the Berlin Philharmonic, and won rave reviews around the world from an enchanted press.

She returned to the United States, where she was hailed as "Cinderella" by the San Francisco and Los Angeles papers as their orchestras clamored for the chance to hire her first. San Francisco won, and she was showered with praise and guest appearances here and all over the world. Yogananda had helped her find her way through his belief in the inner drive and the power of positive thinking through meditation.

> The wind howls like a hammer,
> The night blows cold and rainy,
> My love, she's like a raven
> At my window with a
> broken wing.
>
> BOB DYLAN, *"Love Minus Zero"*

But Dr. Brico had health problems—sinus infections that plagued her her whole life, and she had a drastic surgery that removed tissue from the sinus cavities. In spite of these problems, she toured Europe, conducting Sibelius's orchestra at his request, and conducting in many cities in the United States and Europe as well. In wartime New York she established a women's symphony that played regularly at Carnegie Hall. Everywhere she played she garnered rave reviews.

She had fought long and hard for her position as a conductor—not a woman conductor, but a conductor among
her male peers, equally respected. In New York, she hired
Carnegie Hall with a huge orchestra, and rehearsed at her
own expense to prove to Bruno Walter, Arthur Rubinstein,
and other male conductors that she was up to the job. They
were convinced, and recommended her to orchestras in the
U.S. and Europe.

In 1945 she was invited to Denver to conduct their then-
nonprofessional Denver Symphony. The orchestra loved her
and asked her to come back to Denver—they were turning
professional and would, they said, offer her the job of conductor if she came to Denver. She jumped at the chance and
arrived in Denver with her two Steinway pianos and everything else she owned. The air was dry and her sinuses were
better and she began to fall in love with the mountains, as we
all do!

In a turn of events that would haunt her for years, the
Denver Symphony's board of directors gave the job to Saul
Caston, because, they decided, a woman "could not join the
Cactus Club," an exclusive men's club where much business,
and potential orchestral fundraising, might be done. She had
held blindfolded auditions to prove to the public that a
woman's competence could not be judged by her sex. Now,
once again in Denver, her sex was at issue. She stayed in
Denver, teaching piano and starting her own semiprofes-
sional orchestra.

Nothing could stop this determined woman. She formed another orchestra in Denver, the Denver Businessman's Orchestra, this one with men as well as women, and went on working, touring to conduct in Europe and the U.S., and teaching.

> If you want enlightenment,
> chop wood and carry water.
>
> CHINESE PROVERB

I was fortunate enough to become her piano student in 1949, when I was nine and we had moved to Denver from Los Angeles. She changed my technique, working hard with me for many years. I debuted with her orchestra playing a Mozart concerto, and she told me I could go all the way as a classical pianist. She said I had the hands and the talent, and I believed her. After all, she was internationally known and seemed to know what she was talking about. Even Toscanini paused to pay his respects to Dr. Brico when he came through Denver to conduct in the early fifties. I carried his music to his rehearsal, trailing behind the two of them as they chatted away, feeling like a pampered puppy dog!

I made a movie about Dr. Brico, *Antonia: A Portrait of the Woman,* and it won international praise—it got a spot in the Top Ten Movies of the Year in *Time* magazine, an Academy Award nomination, as well as many other distinctions. After the movie, Dr. Brico returned to conduct many orchestras around the world, including the London Philharmonic and the Mostly Mozart Orchestra in New York. It was after this second wave of her career and success when she told me about Yogananda, and I became a student of his practice of meditation—what a gift she had given me. She advised me to read *Autobiography of a Yogi.* I learned the Yogananda practice, which involves, among other things, disciplines that calm the heart and the nerves, and put one in touch with some great universal energy, or God, if you will.

The way of Self-Realization, as described so eloquently in Yogananda's book and demonstrated in the fast, definite connection I feel building over the years, has brought many promises of healing to fruition. I have a life that is often filled with ecstasy. And I believe all of life can be lived with the positive. It is exhilarating.

Dr. Brico always said that our relationship was what she called karmic, that we had known each other as student and teacher in a previous life, and that we would meet again. Although

A woman came to the wise man of the tribe, her dead child in her arms. "Bring him back to life," she said. "Only if you can bring me a handful of poppy seeds from the house where there is no death. Then I will bring him back from death."

Anonymous

I didn't understand her when I was younger, I now believe that she was absolutely right. I began taking lessons from SRF and doing the "Kriya Yoga." I found it to be the type of meditation that "cut the cake" for me, as I said to my husband. It happened to be thirty years after my first piano lesson with Dr. Brico.

I had been studying piano with Dr. Brico for five years when I met Lingo the Drifter, a raconteur, folksinger, and character-about-town in Denver. It would turn out that he, too, was involved in a form of meditation, one that involved a similar practice—the lifting of the eyes to the forehead—in order to better reach what he and others, including Yoganada, have called Nirvana. But neither with Dr. Brico nor with Lingo did I have discussions about meditation. It was only in later years that I realized both of them had used meditation in their lives—to live through tragedy and difficulty.

Oh! why should the spirit
of mortal be proud?
Like a swift-fleeting meteor,
a fast-flying cloud,
A flash of lightning, a break
of the wave,
He passeth from life to
his rest in the grave.

WILLIAM KNOX, *"Mortality"*

Lingo the Drifter moved to Denver from Chicago in 1954. He had a show on the local Denver FM music and talk radio station, playing and singing the songs of Woody Guthrie and Pete Seeger, telling stories about folk music, and reading Walt Whitman and Longfellow. My father loved the radio show and called him up and asked him over one Sunday afternoon. They became friends, and often he and my father would sit around in our living room, smoking their pipes, talking philosophy, my father singing Rogers and Hart and "Danny Boy" and Lingo singing "This Land Is Your Land" and "The Union Maid." They would talk— about books, about life. I would listen, sometimes quietly, sometimes joining in. My mother would be cooking dinner, and the smell of roast beef and gravy, mashed potatoes and steamed green beans, apple pie and great coffee, would fill the house. Lingo drank my father's whiskey and would often be at the table when dinner was served.

I listened to Lingo's mysterious stories, and was invited along with my mother and father to go up to his log cabin on Lookout Mountain to drink home brew, eat homemade borscht, and swap songs with other singers who belonged to the small and rather elite Denver folklore society.

Studs Terkel, the writer and biographer of American stories, told me later that he had known Lingo in Chicago when Lingo was called Paul somebody. Paul was in Chicago radio, and had lost his wife and a child in a tragic automobile accident. He decided to get lost in the West and headed for Denver. He changed his name to Lingo and never looked back.

I had started to sing folk music before I met Lingo, but again, the coincidence was too real to be imagined—I can hardly separate the time I fell in love with the music from the meeting with Lingo, although I remember the song I heard that sealed the deal—"Barbara Allen" playing on the radio, as sung by Jo Stafford. I had already started singing "Gypsy

Rover," performing the song as my friends Marsha Pinto and Carol Shank danced the story, and had asked my father to get me a guitar so that I could start learning folk music.

But it was after I met Lingo that I knew I would have to give up the piano. I would not be learning the Rachmaninoff piano concerto and I knew I would have to tell Dr. Brico that she would have to forget my playing with her orchestra again. It was a very hard decision. I had played piano from the time I was five, and at fifteen I was studying the great Rachmaninoff Piano Concerto no. 2. Brico was very unhappy that I had decided to throw over Beethoven and Debussy for Woody Guthrie! She thought I was making the wrong decision. Both of us cried, and I was in misery. I was having the first career crisis of my life. But I knew there wasn't room for both Rachmaninoff and Pete Seeger, and that I had to follow my heart.

> The life of the dead consists of being present in the minds of the living.
>
> CICERO, *Orationes*

I remembered Lingo talking about something called the "Dormant Brain Cell Research Foundation." I would later learn that Lingo's dormant brain research ideas basically involved doing the same thing Dr. Brico was doing in her practice—bringing her eyes to the point between the eyebrows and sitting in silence, saying a mantra perhaps, watching her breath. Meditating.

Lingo would explain his philosophy and his outlook on

meditation to my father. He and my father talked about how being blind, as my father was, was simply another way of not seeing the possibilities around you, and my father, overcoming his blindness in all the ways he did, was seeing possibilities all the time. I know Lingo admired Daddy for that, and felt he had found a kindred spirit. Like my father, whose philosophy was one of the positive, the optimistic; and like Dr. Brico, whose salvation was meditation the Yogananda way, Lingo had found a way to live with the difficulties that he experienced, the suicidal thoughts that plagued him after the death of his wife and daughter.

He would talk about charting your emotions—and finding out how to take your body from negativity to a positive place with the breath, and with thought patterns. It was what my dad was doing every time he entered into the sighted world, where he had to have a sense of inner space and peace just in order to walk down the street.

Lingo talked about Nirvana, or being in a place of wild creativity, and how so few people get there. He and my dad would laugh when they talked, giddy with the knowledge that they knew something most people were struggling to find—a sense of happiness, of joy, in spite of blindness, of loss, of the evidence in the world that might contradict their feelings.

Lingo would say that Nirvana was the goal, and that we had to do much more than survive. We had to go deeply into the meditative state to awaken all the other gifts that lay in our minds, beyond the everyday demands of existence. He said if we used more of those brain cells, we would be happier. He felt that without meditation, a person could not engage the energetic thrust toward joy that dwells in every mind and heart. He said that the discipline involved getting the mind hooked up—through meditation and bringing the eyes to the center of the forehead, quieting down, and locking on to the inner silence. That is where meditation begins, and that would lead anyone to bliss. That is where, up there in his hideout on Lookout Mountain, among the pines and under the stars, he practiced and taught the elements of his way of meditating in his school that he founded.

Although Lingo's home brew was very good, and despite the fact that he never refused my father's good whiskey, I never thought of him as either a lush or a drug user. Lingo's secret was an inner, not outer one.

Here, I imagine the connection to my own meditation and prayer practices, for I can trace my joy, my celebration of life, just as Lingo has done, to *The Practice of the Presence of God*, the title of a little book of prayer and meditation by Brother Lawrence, written in the fifteenth century; or by the meditation practice that I learned from Yogananda, with the eyes directed to the center of the forehead, the following of the breath, and the repeating of certain prayers; or to many more simple celebrations of prayer and letting go of trying to control the universe. Or my thoughts!

On KFML in Denver, Lingo sang the songs of Woody

Guthrie and Pete Seeger. His philosophy, he would tell my father, was simple. On the surface, he would appear conformist. Articulate, sophisticated, and an educated mountain man. But under the surface of acceptable, intelligent chatter, he would slip in the values, words, attitudes, and behaviors of the First Amendment to the Constitution, along with his thoughts on the philosophy of life and discussions of civil rights and great truths.

That was in many ways what my father, on his radio show, was doing as well. Giving people something real and positive and healing. Hope, laughter, music. No wonder they became friends!

Lingo was happy when I began to make my way in the professional rounds of coffeehouses and bars where the music of Pete Seeger and Woody Guthrie and, later, Dylan were to be found. But Lingo's true love was the Dormant Brain Cell Research Foundation, and I think that trumped folk music. Or perhaps *was* folk music. Perhaps folk music helped his brain cells as well as his heart.

Over the years I have developed my own graph that tells me what to do to bring about total involvement, joy, celebration, and exuberance in living life. Key to the list is exercise and prayer. If I am not exercising, I will drop toward feelings of depression.

Lingo was also convinced that without meditation, a person could fall into a state of depression that could lead to suicide. He asserted that willpower, or the use of the mind in meditation as a vehicle to bliss, was the answer, and that meditation would unleash the brain cells that would be otherwise dormant in our lives. Dormant, to Lingo, meant unhealthy, and therefore a contributor to depression, anxiety, sadness, preoccupation with dark thoughts, and, finally, death.

> Praising what is lost
> makes the remembrance dear.
>
> WILLIAM SHAKESPEARE,
> *All's Well That Ends Well*

Lingo would say that if your emotions are functioning properly, you are growing. If not, you are dying.

When Lingo was developing his theory of dormant brain cell function, Bob Dylan had not yet come along to tell us that "he who is not busy growing is busy dying." But, actually, Dylan was nearby at least one or two of those summers, working in Crested Butte, Colorado, in 1959, when I was working at the Gilded Garter in Central City. Dylan has told me he came to hear me sing and sat at my feet, and I wonder if he and Lingo ever met, and if, in his extensive reading of books of all kinds, Dylan ever ran across the Dormant Brain Cell Research Foundation!

> But trailing clouds of
> glory do we come
> From God, who is our home.
>
> WILLIAM WORDSWORTH,
> *"Intimations of Immortality"*

Both Lingo the Drifter and Dr. Antonia Brico had found meditation in their lives, and I think, from the vantage point of nearly fifty-five years, that these meditation techniques saved them each from self-destruction. In Dr. Brico's case, meditation helped heal the heartbreak of not being able to conduct as much as she would have liked to. It also healed a sad and abusive childhood at the hands of her foster parents. Lingo used his Dormant Brain Cell Research Foundation and meditation to survive the sudden and tragic loss of his family, as well as continuing to do what he did, such as talk about unpopular ideas during the McCarthy era.

And so my stories about Dr. Brico and Lingo the Drifter come to an end. They are a reminder that there were people around me, my father, my mother, my teachers and mentors, who were propelled, each in their own way, to find means to circumvent thoughts of self-destruction and overcome tragedies and difficulties in their lives. They are powerful examples to me, powerful lessons.

> When the redbird spread
> his sable wing,
> And showed his side of flame;
> When the rosebud ripened
> to the rose,
> In both I read thy name.
>
> RALPH WALDO EMERSON,
> *"Thine Eyes Still Shined"*

I have been shown ways to heal that are not so terribly mysterious, but very practical and reasonable. I would never have found those paths were it not for my past, my mentors, my teachers. And I would not live very long if I did not know these practices *are* my present as well as future.

Treat Affirmations

I will use prayer during the day to steady my thoughts and my emotions.

I will find someone who needs help, and offer my time. Who knows, I might help to save my own life as well as theirs.

I will find myself a haven on earth, a place where, regardless of the state of my mind, my heart can be guided to light and joy.

I will find a place, a room, a chair, a tree, a quiet space in my heart, where I can settle into the conviction that all is for the best and that I am on a path that is concerned with my soul.

I will find a way to rise above pain.

SIX

Thrive

Keep living with your eyes wide open. Don't give in to the temptation to abuse alcohol or other addictive substances to blunt or blur your sadness.

Thrive Affirmations

I will dedicate time today to think of the positive.

I will find someone to help, someone who needs my company, and be there for them.

I will remember that my attitude is everything, that no matter what happens, I can be positive and loving, helpful and hopeful.

I will find a place to be quiet and say thank you to my Higher Power, who has given me life and its joys as well as its sorrows.

I will find goodness in the world, and celebrate it.

I will find goodness in myself, and enlarge upon it; I will remember this tragedy is not personal.

The woods are lovely, dark and deep,
But I have promises to keep,
And miles to go before I sleep,
And miles to go before I sleep.

ROBERT FROST, *"Stopping by Woods on a Snowy Evening"*

IT'S NOT WHAT HAPPENS TO US, BUT OUR ATTITUDE THAT COUNTS

I recently traveled to Vancouver, Canada, to speak at the World Gathering on Bereavement. There were people there from all over the world, people who had lost their sons or daughters, their parents or spouses, to murder or to suicide, to death from disease, and death by both natural and unnatural causes. There was the couple who founded The Compassionate Friends, an organization that has done so much to bring together people whose losses are intolerable, unmentionable, and terrible.

I was there to talk about how I survived the suicide of my son, yet, in the midst of what might have been a dark, sad, sorrowful place and time, I found joy and laughter, tears and hugs; these were people who have truly learned that it is not what happens to you, but your attitude toward it that counts. They express their grief outwardly, in stories and in pictures, often wearing a laminated photograph of a loved one in view on a necklace, or carrying a photograph in their purse or pocket. They listen, absorbing each other's stories, and look into each other's eyes. The looking is healing.

When you have experienced such a loss it is not always the case that others will look into your eyes. It takes courage, that look. To see and to comfort, and to get through the loss and the loneliness—that is the function of friendship, of conferences like these, and of finding people you can talk to and share with. You have to build that bridge of love and understanding so that you can walk in the world again and feel all the feelings that come up. It was a brave and a vital group of people, and I was honored that they had chosen me to speak to them about my own loss.

It was Linda Woods who had suggested I come and talk at the gathering. Linda had heard me speak a couple of years before—at a suicide survivors' conference in New York, I believe. She is about fifty, and was the mother of three before she and her husband, Glenn, lost both boys; one died by his own hand at thirteen; the other, who had been nine at the time of his brother's death, was killed in an automobile accident at the age of sixteen. Linda and Glenn, full of life and passion for reaching out, for leading lives of commitment and continuity, lives rich with friendships and extended family, are a delightful, refreshing couple. They were so kind and so generous to me the day I spent with them at the conference. They provided that instant understanding of what one has gone through, which for me, is a sign of a healing, hopeful life, the kind of life I have strived for in the aftermath of my own tragedy. These people serve as a constant reminder to me of the courage it takes to thrive even when you've endured great loss.

BUT HOW CAN WE GO FORWARD?

That was a question that I explored a lot with the lovely people I met at the World Gathering on Bereavement. Many of us had lists that we referred to every day—lists of things that had healed us, that continue to heal us.

Most days I dwell on my list for some time when I write in my journal. I have to remind myself every day that there are things that make me feel better, and that doing the right things enhances my mood, and makes life better for those around me!

Why not put your own list down on paper and refer to it each morning and then again at the end of the day to see if you have done something related to each item.

My current list reads like this:

- Exercise—a routine that keeps me fit
- Eat Right—avoiding certain foods
- Talk—to my friends
- Write—in my journal
- Practice—an instrument, a skill
- Take Action—make a list, even just a little action
- Work—that is satisfying, productive
- Learn—something new, a game, a song
- Play—see a movie, dance, walk
- Pray—and meditate

RESIST THE URGE TO SELF-MEDICATE

I always speak of the body, mind, and spirit aspects of my recovery, both from alcoholism and from my son's suicide.

> There are the dark days that must be survived, and there is the reality that beckons on the other side of each river of loss.
>
> ANONYMOUS

I make it clear that, although I understand the need for medication at times, and under certain circumstances, I do not and have not had the need to take pills of any kind (except vitamins, of which I take dozens a day!) or use alcohol or drugs of a mood-changing nature, including antidepressants. On my list of things that make me feel better, there are exercise and meditation, friends and talk therapy (I still see a therapist from time to time and would like to see my insurance company pay for the visits, just as they have paid for the visits with my physical therapist for my shoulder replacement).

When my turn came to talk at this gathering of about a thousand people, I was feeling nervous. We had had our meal, and I had sat and eaten and laughed and been a part of the evening, which I don't always do. I usually feel that I need to be alone to both collect my thoughts and also to make sure that my voice is clear, which means I usually don't eat dinner before I speak. I want to be calm, collected, and focused and therefore usually save the talking, the singing, and the socializing until after my speaking is done.

> What is the secret to daily living? Simple. It is daily dying.
>
> *Joe and Charlie*
> *Big Book Study*

NEGATIVITY IS AN ADDICTION

This night, however, I felt that I was truly among friends, speaking not for myself, but for everyone there who had gone through terrible times and come out a person who can relate to others, that it seemed like I would benefit more from being at the table with Glenn and Linda and their friends, many of whom they had known for fifteen or twenty years. I wanted to be among loving people.

I always sing a bit when I talk, breaking into the familiar songs people know and I feel at ease with. I sing a little of "Both Sides Now," as everyone has heard me sing that song over the years; I sing a little of the Kerry Dancers or one of the Rogers and Hart songs my father used to play on his radio show. Breaking into melody from a standstill, so to speak, is part of what I love to do; it

> Alcohol distorts our perception of reality and eventually acts as a depressant. God's Spirit in our hearts clarifies our understanding and gives us enthusiasm and deep joy.
>
> HAZELDEN MEDITATIONS, *Food for Thought: Daily Meditations for Overeaters*

puts people at ease, and me as well. Then I tell my own story, including some of the background I feel would be helpful to share—that alcohol, in my own case, and my son's case, played a pivotal role in my suicide attempt, and my son's successful suicide.

For me, drugs and alcohol were always the answer when I was in the throes of my disease, and at one time or another I had used every drug, every drink, in the book. Like Alice in Wonderland, I took one bottle to make me small, another to make me tall. I was tall, small, vanished, little, big, conscious, unconscious. I went with the prescription I was given, falling down the rabbit holes, cowering when the Queen scolded, playing the fool at the tea party, flaunting and then regretting my bigness, my smallness, my very existence.

I WILL NOT TAKE MY LIFE TODAY

I had been sober for thirteen years when my son died. My sobriety, like everyone's, had come at a very high price. To drink again, and to drug again, would mean I might very well join my son in his final answer. I could not afford to do that.

Each and every day, I would repeat over and over in my prayers, "I will not drink today. I will not drug today. I will not commit suicide today."

It was that simple, and that clear.

I could not, and would not, go back on that terrible dark path that I had trod for the many years I had been drinking, before the light dawned on my life, before the miracle of sobriety had come, before whatever hand exists in Heaven had reached down to pull me from the fire I had started and fanned, throwing all my belongings, all my dreams, all my promise, and all my hopes into the flames. I could not go back. As you navigate the narrow and winding path out of your own grief, I beg you to be careful not to allow yourself to use alcohol and drugs to medicate against the pain, for it will not work. The only way to soothe the hurt is to face it with a clear and unmedicated mind. Then, when the clouds lift, you will be able to see the sky, feel the dawn.

MAGICAL CURES

I read recently that the FDA barred the agency's top expert from testifying at a public hearing that certain antidepressants can cause children to become suicidal, because it found his conclusion alarmist. There were mixed opinions about Paxil, the drug under scrutiny. The controversy had its start when GlaxoSmithKline sought an extension on its patents on Paxil.

This in itself might easily suggest that it is time to look more closely at the idea that has gained popularity in recent years that all suicides are a result of depression, and that all depression must necessarily be treated with antidepressants and other drugs. In many cases insurance companies refuse to pay for longer-term therapy, so consequently I believe that doctors prescribe antidepressants rather quickly. Just as those of us who have gone through painful loss and confronted the urge to use illegal substances or alcohol to ease our sorrow, I believe we must be wary of drugs that

Remind yourself constantly that you have nothing to deal with but your own thoughts. Write it down where you will see it often. Have it on your desk. Hang it in your pocketbook. Write it on your soul. It will transform your life. It will lead you out of the land of Egypt and out of the House of Bondage. It will bring you to God.

EMMET FOX, *Around the Year with Emmet Fox*

we are told will cure depression. They may help, but you must also use other practices that are vital as well.

THE INSURANCE COMPANIES— WITH US OR AGAINST US?

One thing that we are all fighting for here in the awakened mental health arena is parity for mental health costs—we want the insurance companies to pay on deaths by suicide; to pay for talk therapy, not just pills; to let our doctors and our professional health-care advisors lead us to what we need, and not have to adjust our medications or our treatments to what the insurance companies will or will not pay for. It is time for mental and physical health to come back together, for the body, mind, and spirit to be reunited.

Recently a Senate bill has been proposed that would provide thirty million dollars for the study of suicide. The prevailing philosophy, i.e., that drugs are the answer in every case, seems to be the driving force behind this bill—no broader psychological or behavioral modification techniques are being suggested—although there exists now, thanks to Senator Harkin (who we last heard a great deal about when he was a contender for the 1992 presidential slot), a section of the National Institutes of Health that is dedicated to the study of alternative medicine. And we are now seeing large medical resources directed toward alternative treatments at major hospitals in the United States, including a substantial wing of Beth Israel Hospital in New York City, where one can receive acupuncture, talk therapy, chiropractic treatment, herbal remedies, massage, and other techniques that are known to cure illness that Western medicine has often failed to treat.

> Suicide is an act of hope;
> the soul who commits suicide
> cannot bear the place in which it
> finds itself and reaches out
> for something better.
>
> CATHOLIC PRIEST AT AN
> AA/ALANON RETREAT
> IN COLORADO

I prefer to call alternative medicine *complementary*, as it is not a stand-alone arena of medicine, but a complement to allopathic, or Western medicine, which I use for many things.

I propose that part of the thirty-million-dollar budget for the study of suicide be applied to alternative medicine and its use with people at risk.

BE AWARE OF YOUR VULNERABILITY

We have to protect ourselves in our grief. Many of us may become statistics of suicide if we do not find a way through our grief that reveals strength and courage enough for us to go on into a different, healthy mental and physical state.

The statistics for death from suicide in the USA are staggering—thirty-five thousand people, approximately nineteen thousand of them adolescents, die by their own hands every year. Each leaves an average of ten survivors—family and friends—three hundred and fifty thousand people who are fighting to survive a terrible, and for the most part misunderstood, malady, and many of whom also are more prone to suicide themselves. And they wage a fight of body, mind, and spirit against a further enemy—the enemy of taboo. We are often tempted not to talk about it, think about it, write about it, and then we find that when we don't talk about it, our secrets can cause us deep emotional and physical pain, and, in some cases, may kill us.

> If you are to go from one mountain to another, there is a valley between them through which you must walk.
>
> DR. ROBERT SCHULLER

The drama of the suicide resides permanently in the survivors. We are the ones who must fight a battle we did not ask for. We struggle to open our hearts to forgiveness and to life itself. As suicide survivors, we have to find ways not only to survive, but also to thrive.

I attempted suicide at the age of fourteen. I was fortunate to find a very wise therapist in my twenties who talked me through many of the troubling issues that led to that attempt. I am also an alcoholic who thought of suicide in all of my twenty-three years of drinking. I do not drink today, but I know that active drug addicts and alcoholics are much more prone to suicide than

> Our life's work is to use what we have been given to wake up.
>
> PEMA CHODRON,
> *The Wisdom of No Escape*

their sober counterparts. My son was an alcoholic, and he took his life during a relapse after seven years of sobriety.

I do not take any medication of any kind for depression, although I have suffered from depression from a young age. I believe that the holistic approach has given me clarity and the power to recover and I share the means I used, which do not include drugs, in *Sanity & Grace*, as well as in this book.

> Ring the bells that still can ring.
> Forget your perfect offering.
> There is a crack in everything.
> That's how the light gets in.
>
> LEONARD COHEN, *"Anthem"*

"Where does it hurt, and how can I help?" Getting treatment for the pain can be difficult, as insurance companies often refuse to pay for long-term talk therapy. Therefore, the leap to medication is often a first step, where perhaps it might be a second or third step, but certainly not the only way to treat the many symptoms that surround the suicidal mind.

> Thence we came forthe to
> see the stars again.
>
> DANTE, *The Divine Comedy*

THRIVING

It was Easter again, the lilies and the promise of new life. After Clark's death I had a dream of him that was so vivid and so real that I said to a friend that it was like a visitation, not just a dream. In this dream, he came to me saying, "Mother, why are you crying?" In church the other day the bishop tells the story of the celestial beings who came to Mary after Jesus had disappeared from the tomb. "Why are you crying?" they asked her. And Jesus said the same thing to Mary when he appeared to her. "I am with God," Jesus said. When I told this to the dean, my friend Jim Morton, he shook his head. He is a gentle and kind man, a man who embraces spirituality and healing where it comes.

He said, "If all of this isn't true, we're in big trouble!"

I thought of my own death that day of the resurrection. What I would want to say to these loved ones I left behind. "Why are you crying?" I would say. I would try to help them, sending them all my love and support. I know that is what my son is doing, sending his spirit, his power, his prayers, to help me through this veil of tears. His own

> Joy is like a soft spring rain that allows us to lighten up, to enjoy ourselves, and therefore it's a whole new way of looking at suffering.
>
> PEMA CHODRON,
> *The Wisdom of No Escape*

pain is over now, and that is something I can celebrate, for I don't wish that pain on anyone, let alone my son. He is at peace.

I pray to understand that my son is out of his pain and that my tears must be of joy, and of surrender.
I pray that I can go on from day to day, celebrating the good things and dwelling on the positive.

Thrive Affirmations

Today I will look for the best in everyone, including myself.

I will do the work, and let go of the results.

I will have a positive attitude no matter what.

I will resist the urge to self-medicate. I will be clear and present for my healing.

I will watch my thoughts each day for negativity and when I find it, seek to change my thoughts to the positive.

I will seek the help I need from friends and professionals.

I will look for ways to help others for that will help me as well.

SEVEN

Transcend

We are in the process of learning how to live again—with joy, with commitment to expressing all of ourselves: our hopes, our aspirations, our life that is still to be lived—in celebration of ourselves as well as of those we love, those who are in our lives and those who are no longer with us. You must. Live a life of joy, abundance, and forgiveness.

Transcend Affirmations

I will get up in the morning with energy and optimism.

I will find someone to love in my life—a pet, a new person.

I will start something new, something beautiful. Perhaps it will be painting, perhaps a poem.

I will smile when I want to frown.

I will find a new spiritual discipline, perhaps finding ways to make life easier or happier for others, giving of my time.

I will listen to music, and perhaps go to the museum more often.

I will Transcend death.

Rise up, my love, my fair one, and come away.
For lo, the winter is past, the rain is over and gone;
The flowers appear on the earth;
the time of the singing of birds is come . . .

Song of Solomon 2:10–12

MIRACLES ARE HAPPENING
ALL AROUND US

The *New American Heritage Dictionary* defines *transcend* as "to pass beyond a human limit; an emotion that transcends understanding; to rise above or across; rising above common thought or ideas; exalted; mystical."

If you are given the terrible presence of catastrophic loss and grief, overcoming it may prove to be the hardest journey you will ever make. But when you start upon your journey of healing, you will also be given opportunities you might never have been offered if loss had not come to you, suddenly or slowly; opportunities to climb your own Everest; to build your own Chautauqua; to sail your own sea in your own six-masted vessel; to possess the priceless. The cost is high; nothing in your life will teach you so much, or ask so much of you in return.

None of us welcomes this journey, but if we want to live fully and blessedly and joyfully, and be of service to others, we have only two choices—take the ride, or live in landscapes where your dreams will not have the courage to bloom and your ideas and life force will dwindle from lack of sun and soil. Catastrophic loss is big-time, a Ph.D. of life, an advanced degree in living. In order to help your soul bloom through loss, you must be willing to dig, deep and far. Being present for the journey is your only hope of getting to your destination.

> Miracles are not contrary to nature but only contrary to what we know about nature.
>
> ST. AUGUSTINE

The bird singing in the trees, the flowers blooming, and the light coming in the window—we just don't call them miracles. Matisse said that the most exciting image for him was a half-open door—the expectation, the mystery, the wonder of that open door. For what might come into the room? The miraculous. We must learn, if we are to thrive, to look for the miracle everywhere, the open door through which can come our salvation, our remarkable mysterious solution. It is around every corner, in every season. Beauty in our lives is a miracle; our breathing, our sleep, are miracles. The dreams that haunt us, that heal us, the food that nurtures us, all miracles. We are souls living in a body that functions, does for us without our thinking. Miracles. What more proof do we need?

In loss and grief, we have to keep hoping, for that is the miracle. We have to hope for peace for ourselves, for the ones who are gone. We yearn for rest, for forgiveness when we think we might have erred. For forgiveness of others when we know others have harmed us. For the energy to do what we have to do. All these are miracles when they come, the waking with calm instead of a wildly beating heart and a wildly flying mind. The good health that will follow a period of depression and grief, the results of our efforts to cleanse and remember, to be free of guilt, of remorse. These moments of clarity and peace are miracles.

> White wings, they
> never grow weary,
> they carry me cheerily
> over the sea;
> night falls, I dream of my dearie,
> I spread out my white wings
> and fly home to thee.
>
> BANKS WINTER, *"White Wings"*

We pray for the lifting of negativity, of the healing of a deep wound felt in the marrow of our beings. When relief comes, we feel the miracle, and we want to celebrate it. When the dawn comes, feel the miracle. When the smile comes after the storm of anger, feel the miracle. When the

> God will pardon me,
> it is his trade.
>
> HEINRICH HEINE, *The Oxford Dictionary of Quotations*

wind dies, when the sea calms, when the sun shines, feel the miracle.

Tell yourself that appreciating the dance of the seasons of nature, in her physical and emotional episodes, is to be witnessing a miracle. Coach yourself to appreciate where you are going, where you have been. For you have been down into the deep well where the darkness can only be followed by light. You have lost someone you could not possibly lose and still live. You have seen the things that the myths of ancient Greece reflect, that the parables of olden times remember; you are writing your own history of experience that will follow. Teach yourself that of all the experiences in the world, your own is the crucial one for you. You must live it to the fullest, and for that you will bear witness to your own destructions and your own miracles.

Science has proved over and over that a bumblebee cannot fly. The wings of a bumblebee are too tiny and its body too big. And yet, over and over, the bumblebee flies, for it believes it can fly. It hasn't heard the experts' opinions about bumblebees.

Joe and Charlie Big Book Study

Each of us is living out the Bible of our journey, and each has a unique story to tell.

Let yourself in on the secret; miracles are happening to us every day, all of our lives.

For eleven years, from the age of thirty to the age of forty-one, I suffered from bulimia (an eating disorder in which the symptom is binging, then purging, vast quantities of food—predominantly sugar and carbohydrates). At the age of forty I was on the brink of committing (or trying to commit) suicide. I should have been happy—I was sober—but I could not stop the food addiction. It was one of the darkest periods of my life, and I was filled with shame about the condition I was in. I did not find much written about bu-

> O month of Flowering,
> months of Metamorphosis,
> May without cloud and June
> that was stabbed,
> I shall never forget the
> lilac and the roses,
> Nor those whom spring
> has kept in its folds.
>
> Louis Aragon, *The Oxford Dictionary of Quotations*

limia; in fact I thought I had invented the practice! Little did I know that girls in sports, in groups of peers at high school and college, and on their own, I imagine, had been doing this long after the Romans invented it. I was told that there probably would be no help or understanding of the problem in the usual weight-loss programs and groups devoted to finding release from addictions. I didn't know then that bulimia is rampant among young women who are concerned about the shape of their bodies and addicted to control, as I now know I am!

I was ready to walk in front of a bus on the last day of my binging and purging. I had tried to kill myself once. This time I would succeed, I knew. I had no more options. I went to a church near my home to find a group I thought met there, and couldn't find one. I was beyond despair.

So I asked again, on my knees, and I made my way to another church, where there was supposed to be a spiritual meeting about food.

It was a Saturday afternoon, and at the church I met a woman who told me what to do—basically, to eat three meals a day and two snacks, to call her every day and tell her what I was going to eat, and to pray. "Pray your ass off," she told me. "You might as well, nothing else has worked."

Praise and Blame
Pleasure and Pain
Fame and Disrepute
Gain and Loss
Success and failure

ANGUTTARA NIKAYA,
The Eight Vicissitudes of Life

The next morning the terrible addiction and its burden of shame and guilt (and teeth problems!) was lifted. I found the help I needed. Through friends who knew about my problem, I found another who had the same problem and had been able to kick the habit.

That was nearly twenty-four years ago. Today, I wonder, what causes a ray of hope to appear? I had walked a path of faith, believing even when I saw no proof, that God was there somewhere and would help me if I asked. But I had been desperate, and ill. Help had come to me. Hope, and unseen blessings, were now visible in my life.

One of the many things I appreciated about our long-lost Princess Diana was that she talked publicly about her bulimia. She said her doctor had said to her, "If you can keep your food down, your life will change."

Jane Fonda says in her autobiography that girls with eating disorders account for a good percentage of the total number of deaths in women between the ages of fourteen and twenty-four—and among those deaths, many are suicides.

> Where life conquered death,
> No other solution would do.
>
> ANONYMOUS

I was shocked at the press's lack of attention to the issue of eating disorders in relation to Terri Schiavo's death. According to the medical records released during the dispute over whether or not her husband had the right to let doctors end her life, Schiavo had had an eating disorder (bulimia, or anorexia, the flip side of this illness), which can cause, among other illnesses, loss of consciousness as a result of low levels of potassium and a compromised pH balance. This is common with eating disorders, and the fact that it was overlooked or ignored

> Without absolute death,
> there is no creation.
>
> KRISHNAMURTI

in discussions surrounding her fate says a great deal about the public's lack of education and understanding of how dangerous eating disorders can be.

Heart attack and stroke can also result, as was the case in the death of Karen Carpenter, who had had a history of anorexia and died of a heart attack resulting from her eating disorder.

For some reason, after being able to share this terrible problem with another person, the next morning the nightmare of my bulimia was over. I have never looked back and always thanked God, and that kind friend, for showing me the way. She had been where I had been and come through it. She told me how she had done it.

LIKE CURES LIKE

When I talk about my problems with someone who has been there, we can help each other.

These days, I look for the chance to learn more about how to live with the fire and the energy and the life force that is all around me at all times. It has always been there. Julia Cameron, author of *The Artist's Way*, told me recently that she saw some of our family histories of addiction and talent as "So much passion looking for a place to land."

> There is only one liberty: to come to terms with death. After which, everything is possible.
>
> ALBERT CAMUS

We talked about how it is hard to deal with, as it comes with a huge amount of drama that surrounds life's ebb and flow, its joys and its tragedies. Today, in the light of my experience, this driving force seems to be more precious, dearer to me than ever, and I must try every day not to buy into my own soap opera.

But I try every day to be hopeful, positive, and loving. I try every day to find the infinite space in my soul, that place where all troubles and triumphs burn with an everlasting flame of divine truth, the place where I am at peace and my heart sings with joy for the everlasting, never-changing spirit of life itself, where love returns and is reborn, overcoming death.

> Transcendence. It happens all around us. Every day.

Sometimes, though we have no way of understanding why, a terrible thing may have an outcome that can be said in some way to be helpful, healing, and life-changing for those who are left behind. War, of course, is tragic for man, and sometimes in ways that seem unnatural, even for war.

I learned recently that one soldier in Iraq has made a difference I am sure he would never have dreamed of making.

Specialist Thomas John Sweet, the son of Liz Sweet, was twenty-three when he took his life in the spring of 2005 in Iraq. He told his superiors of his concerns. He was then sent for evaluation while on duty in Iraq; his complaints

> The old fashioned function of intimate friendship— of sharing, of the power of one plus one—can heal.
>
> A MENTOR

had been dismissed, and he had subsequently, after an argument with a superior officer over a disciplinary action, died by his own hand.

According to the *New York Times* of June 3, 2005, in an unprecedented ceremony at Arlington National Cemetery, his mother, Liz, "helped lay a wreath honoring soldiers killed in Iraq, including her 23-year-old son T.J. His photograph hung below the wreath on a ribbon Mrs. Sweet had fashioned in red, white and blue, a rare public tribute to a soldier who had taken his own life."

There should have been a star and a huge banner over Liz Sweet's small, lone figure there at Arlington, along with all the other heroes of the battles of the past centuries. Probably for the first time, suicide was being recognized as a part of the human experience, cause for inclusion, the casket carried not over closed gates, but across hallowed, sacred ground, where the bodies of thousands of other heroes lie buried.

In the midst of terrible loss and tragedy, Liz Sweet triumphed. She rose above her sorrow to make sure her son's death was not in vain, that other survivors might have her

> Much is said today of the horror of war between nations; but I tell you that the private wars in the darkness of the human consciousness are no less violent and alarming, and they eventually become manifest in injury to oneself as well as to others.
>
> FROM *Letters of the Scattered Brotherhood*, EDITED BY MARY STRONG

courage; she stepped not down, into the darkness, but forward, into the light.

SEE THE MIRACLE EVERYWHERE

I hope that these practices, learned from my own experiences as well as the experience and writings of other survivors, will be of value. These were the seven gifts without which I could not have survived this journey. I wanted to tell you about them, to help you on the path I have traveled.

May your life be full of pleasure and kindness and appreciation of your gifts. You deserve it, and the one who left you suddenly, sadly, deserves no less.

> God is . . . Life . . . Truth . . . Love . . . Intelligence . . . Soul . . . Spirit . . . Principle. God has every quality of personality except limitation.
>
> EMMET FOX, *Around the Year with Emmet Fox*

In a way, you are living two lives now. May this book help you, and your family, and your ancestors, who might be lost but should never be forgotten.

Transcend Affirmations

I will make a determined effort to see the power and healing of recovery.

I will fill my time with hopeful activities to keep me focused on the positive. I know that I can do more than survive this and I will make every effort to see the light instead of the dark.

I will find someone to help and tell them how I am doing and assure them that they can make it through this difficult time.

I will pray and make a gratitude list of what is good in my life and focus on that rather than my loss.

I will bless my loved one who is gone, bless myself, as well as my friends and my enemies. I will understand that doubt and fear are my enemies and live in the presence of hope. I know I can get through anything with the help of my spirit and my faith. I can and will Transcend.

Acknowledgments

I would like to thank my publisher, Joel Fotinos. His support has meant a great deal to me. I love working with him and have benefited from his insight and willingness to engage in not just publishing, but editing, thinking through the books, and helping frame their shape.

Many thanks to Sara Carder, my superb editor, who has added so much to this book, in time and thought, ideas and views in this difficult journey. Special thanks to Kathryn Kimball for her help also.

Thanks to Katherine De Paul, for all the energy, ideas, and help in putting together everything that is needed to carry on the way that helps me write and concertize.

Thanks to the wonderful design team at Tarcher, for another beautiful cover, and to Meighan Cavanaugh, who designed such a beautiful book, and to copy editor Leda Scheintaub.

Acknowledgments

Thanks also to Perry Steinberg and Michael Rosenberg at APB. You do a great job!

Thanks to Tarcher, my publisher, who has published my books with a care and concern so rare these days.

I am grateful to my husband, Louis Nelson, and our granddaughter, Hollis; and to my siblings—Holly, David, Michael, and Denver; and to my mother, Marjorie, and stepfather, Robert.

To all of those who have suffered terrible losses and shared their recoveries with me. I am indebted to you for showing me how to live today.

Disasters may well change us deeply, but they will pass. We must keep to our deeper convictions and remember our goals. Whether we remain ash or become the phoenix is up to us.

—*Ming-Dao Deng, 365 Tao: Daily Meditations*

90942